Sporting Excellence

Optimising Sports Performance Using NLP

Ted Garratt

Crown House Publishing Limited

First published in the UK by

Crown House Publishing Limited
Crown Buildings
Bancyfelin
Carmarthen
SA33 5ND
Wales

First published 1999

British Library of Cataloguing-in-Publication Data
A catalogue entry for this book is available
from the British Library.

ISBN 1899836268

Printed and bound in Wales by
WBC Book Manufacturers,
Waterton Industrial Estate,
Bridgend, Mid Glamorgan.

Dedication

This book is dedicated to Cathy
who provides all the foundations.

Table Of Contents

Acknowledgements

In putting this book together there are many people who contributed in lots of different ways.

I would like to thank all the sportspeople who were generous enough to give their time or provide quotes, in particular Dean Richards and Kevin Keegan.

Among the NLP community there are many people who have assisted me either by training or influence. In particular I would like to thank Ian McDermott, Joseph O'Connor, Robert Dilts, Tad James, Shelle Rose Charvet, John Seymour and Miles Peacock for all their positive influence.

Finally I would like to thank the people at Crown House Publishing for being so helpful and supportive.

Preface

Over the last thirty years the focus of attention in sport has shifted dramatically. The traditional ways of building up to a major event, the immediate preparation beforehand, the attitude displayed during the event, and the analysis carried out afterwards, have altered beyond all recognition. It is no longer enough to simply turn up, compete and go home again.

During the same period a similar shift has occurred in most other walks of life: in business where the whole approach is more rigorous; in education when people are preparing for examinations; even in politics where expediency and muddling through become harder to maintain.

So what has contributed towards these shifts? Undoubtedly the pace of life is quicker and the stakes higher. The consequences of failure are more dramatic, careers are made and broken more quickly, and burnout takes a higher toll, and at a younger age. The media attention, focused both on the person and on the performance, means that the effects of success and failure are given greater meaning and substance, creating even more pressure to get things right more quickly.

Developments in the field broadly labelled as sports psychology have mirrored this evolution. Virtually every individual or team has their own coach or fitness guru, coupled with an individual training and development programme. Great attention is paid to diet, relaxation, fitness, mental preparation and many other aspects in order to achieve a greater possibility of success.

Corresponding with these developments has been the advent of NLP which stands for Neuro-Linguistic Programming. NLP was created by Richard Bandler (a mathematician and student of psychology) and John Grinder (a linguist). Their choice of name has probably created more confusion and debate than they ever intended, but each aspect of this name does have particular importance.

Neuro refers to how the brain processes actually work.

Linguistic refers to the way our experiences are represented by the use of language, both externally in communication with others and internally in self-talk.

Programming refers to the specific patterns and programmes of behaviour and thoughts that we follow, to produce specific results.

We all use well-established strategies and patterns of behaviour in order to live our lives effectively, e.g. when driving a car, carrying out home improvements or writing a report. Most of these strategies and patterns are unconscious, i.e. we do them automatically, without thinking. It is very hard, for example, to consciously consider and act on every single thought and action required to drive a car (think back to how difficult this was when you were first learning to drive).

It would not be possible to live our lives if we had to consciously think about every thought and action we undertake. It is the patterns of thought and behaviour that happen unconsciously that are encompassed by the word 'programming'.

From a sportsperson's point of view, these patterns are of enormous importance, because they determine not only the physical actions we carry out, but also the thought processes that lie behind our actions. These thought processes may be beneficial, and may lead us to great sporting victories, but they may also be negative and may inhibit our performance.

NLP allows us to get inside our minds, analyse these programmes and then change them. Obviously, in sport, these changes can be measured and monitored.

NLP also allows us to analyse the strategies – both conscious and unconscious – that successful people use, and to adopt aspects of these for ourselves.

In a sporting context this does not mean that every footballer can be an Alan Shearer or every cricketer a Brian Lara. But it does mean that by using some of their key strategies, all of us can substantially improve our game.

To date NLP has been used mainly in the business, self-development and therapy fields. However, aspects of it have been included already within sport, in areas such as mental preparation, dealing with limiting beliefs and building on successful performances.

This book is intended to help sportspeople of all descriptions, and at all levels, without any prior knowledge or training in NLP, to have fun playing with the techniques and substantially improve their, and their team's, performance.

Introduction

I can do anything I want with the power of my mind.

Mark McGuire, St. Louis Cardinals,
on breaking the baseball home-run record.

The American soldier, Colonel George Hall, was held prisoner in Vietnam for a number of years. He was kept in difficult physical conditions where it was hard to stay fit and certainly impossible to play his favourite game, golf. In order to occupy his mind and keep his sanity he played a round of golf over his favourite course back home, *inside his head*, at least once a day over the five-and-a-half-year period he was held captive. This was in spite of being kept in solitary confinement most of the time in a cell 8½ feet x 8½ feet.

On departing for Vietnam he had played off a four handicap. Five-and-a-half years later, on his return, he was asked to play a round with some friends. To their amazement, and in spite of his weakened physical condition, he immediately played to his original handicap. When they expressed their amazement and said that he had not played for five-and-a-half years he told them that, on the contrary, he had played mentally every day over that period and knew every blade of grass, every bunker and every shot he had ever played.

Source: *The Psychology of Winning* Tape

This story has entered into legend and illustrates a key point: provided that mental practice is made as real as possible and sustained over a sufficient period, it becomes generative. This simply means that it becomes easier and more useful. This is one of those occasions where it is true that PRACTICE MAKES PERFECT.

As we will see later in the book, practice actually doesn't always make perfect. A lot of us struggle with physical practice because it is based upon inappropriate habits, rhythms and methods. The interesting thing about mental preparation is that the same rules apply, but we can solve the issue inside our heads before carrying out the actual physical practice. Therefore it can be extremely useful to have a positive role model in some specific aspects of our mental or physical performance.

In 1991 Steve Backley won virtually everything he entered. Then came the World Championships where he didn't even qualify. When asked why this occurred, he responded that he 'couldn't hear the music' (a classic NLP response). Two weeks later he won a competition in Sheffield, against the same opponents. His analysis of this victory was that 'he had operated from an altered mental state and that the mind is incredibly powerful and the body follows.'

Source: *Equinox* TV Programme

The fear of failure, even with occasional sportspeople, should never be underestimated. In many walks of life additional stress is caused as much by the fear of failure or looking silly as by actually trying something and dealing with the consequences. This is why the practical part of the book offers a variety of techniques for dealing with disempowering beliefs and developing more useful and positive ones.

However, this is not a book about positive thinking. I remember talking to a cricketer just prior to the start of the new season when he was looking to establish himself in the first team of his county for the first time. In the first game he knew that he was due to face Curtly Ambrose, then the number one fast bowler in the world.

To prepare himself for making his breakthrough he bought a book on positive thinking and read it avidly. When I happened to meet him at a lunch he told me how his approach was going to be not to allow the bowler to intimidate him and try not simply to survive, but to hit every ball for a four or six.

Readers with an NLP background will have noted the mixed use of language that the cricketer used. He was at least as concerned with what he was *not* going to do as with what he *was* going to do. Also, the outcome he had set himself was unrealistic and to a large extent out of his control. He had not planned for dealing with factors such as the bowler himself (in this case a significant issue), and the fielders. Also, I felt that he could possibly put himself both physically and mentally in some danger.

Imagine if his plan worked initially, and he actually managed to score a series of boundaries off Curtly Ambrose. All the evidence was that Ambrose would respond to the assault, and that the response could have interesting implications for the batsman, both in the short and long-term!

Without wishing to inhibit his enthusiasm (and bearing in mind that this was a chance encounter), I discussed with him what he could actually deal with and be responsible for, i.e. responding to a bouncer, playing late, playing a bad shot. I pointed out that how he handled these issues would ultimately determine whether he succeeded as a cricketer. His response was that he preferred the more gung-ho approach which had been in the book on positive thinking, as the benefit would be more immediate.

This conversation provided food for thought. It was a complete coincidence that I, with my background, had sat next to him at lunch. Obviously I didn't want to damage his beliefs regarding his new approach. Also the social limitations of the lunch meant that the conversation had been extremely fragmented. I wondered whether I could have done more, but decided that there was very little more I could have done.

Over the next few weeks I watched the batsman's progress with interest. In the game against Northamptonshire he made 17 runs, but stood very little chance against Ambrose.

Monitoring his progress over the season, I noticed that a similar pattern occurred. He would get in and make a few runs against bowlers who weren't famous but, as soon as he came up against someone famous, he was out very quickly. These incidents occurred three years ago. The batsman in question never did establish himself in his county's first team, is no longer on their books, and now plays League cricket.

The purpose of this story is not to debunk positive thinking. Rather it is to underline that personal change in sport (as in life) is not always a matter of a quick fix, although occasionally one incident can change someone permanently, e.g. a win against a much higher-ranked opponent may create a breakthrough.

The picture I have tried to paint in this section is one of a planned, focused evolution in improvement in performance, building on increasingly successful results and enjoying the process. One of the wonderful things about sport is that normally progress can be measured either individually, collectively or both.

How To Use This Book

The purpose of this book is practical. Its test will be the day-to-day use it is put to. Although it could be read straight through, its subject-matter and content lend themselves more to 'dipping in' to find something useful to use.

Although some of the language or jargon used in NLP can require a dictionary of its own, this is not a book aimed at people with prior knowledge of NLP. Its prime focus is sportspeople at all levels and from all sports, irrespective of current ability. Some of you may well recognise that a number of techniques you already use have their origins in NLP.

The important issues are the relevance of the techniques, their ease of application and their usefulness. If some of you find that you wish to go deeper and acquire some formal NLP training, information can be obtained from:

The Association For NLP
PO Box 78
Stourbridge
West Midlands
DY8 4ZJ
Telephone: 01384 443935

The amateur or occasional sportsperson, who is possibly less used to trying out mental techniques, can focus on one specific issue at a time, e.g. better mental preparation or managing stress and anxiety. Choose a technique (or two) and try it for a period of about four to five weeks, longer if the sport is played only once a week.

This is actually a very important issue. Research into developing skills and behaviours (or eliminating bad habits) shows that for a pattern to become ingrained as a natural process, it needs to be worked on for a minimum of four weeks. This applies to all aspects of personal change, e.g. stopping nail-biting, learning a new skill, etc. This is to allow the process to become unconscious and to get past the just-using-willpower stage to allow the new pattern to be absorbed naturally.

Provided the person has practised regularly over this period, the new skill or behaviour will start to become habitualised.

Another key point in using this book is to suspend judgement and to be willing to try something new, or something that initially seems strange or bizarre. One of the common reasons for our becoming stuck is that we stubbornly stick with what we know or have been used to. This book offers some new approaches to try in our search for the difference that makes the difference.

Section One

Background To Sporting Excellence

Chapter 1

A Brief History Of Psychology In Sport

Nowadays nearly every sportsperson mentions some aspects of sports psychology in an interview. Every report on a game or contest, every article written, also touches the subject to some degree or other. This pattern has increased in the last few years and seems to be accelerating.

What makes this remarkable is that, as a field in its own right, sports psychology is a comparatively recent phenomenon. There are many reasons for this. The amount of media exposure that sport now gets is a big factor. Dedicated sports channels are now available. Every incident is replayed from as many different angles as possible. Panels of guests (most of whom were never subjected to the same degree of scrutiny) debate and argue over everything that has taken place. Professional sportspeople are interviewed immediately after their greatest victory or most humiliating defeat. This analysis is also carried out by managers and coaches who use all sorts of vaguely psychological language to explain team or individual strengths, or apparent losses of form.

Having noted all of this, it is interesting that there are still very few true sports psychologists operating in Britain (unlike in America). One reason is that many people do not understand what psychology (let alone sports psychology) is, or what it can and cannot do.

Many players will consult a sports psychologist because they want to win – at all costs. This then places the sports psychologist in a dilemma, if the victory is to be achieved to the detriment of the player's overall psychological wellbeing. Therefore most sports psychologists choose to concentrate rather on improving performance and the psychological wellbeing of the sportsperson they are dealing with.

In the USA the sixties produced a number of books and research reports. These were taken up avidly by sportspeople, managers and coaches. A vein had been struck, and this started to be mined, although slowly at first. Books on sport started to appear that, though not necessarily written by psychologists, carried the momentum forward. Perhaps the most famous of these is *Run To Daylight,* which was written by the well-known American Football coach, Vince Lombardi, and it is still worth a read today.

Lombardi is still quoted today, and many of his expressions, such as 'winning isn't everything, but wanting to is', have passed into sporting legend. This, and other books that followed, carried forward the momentum that the sports psychologists were also creating and made it become an avalanche. Following this, and again mainly in the USA, a wide variety of organisations and societies were created in order to further develop and monitor this expanding subject. Many of these became warring factions which, however, did not seem to hinder the growth and interest in the field. This was because sportspeople were looking for anything that worked and helped. However, it did result in the field becoming split into specialist areas, something again that caused some confusion to potential users.

Nowadays the topic, though still not widely understood, is becoming accepted more and more at all levels. Many fans and spectators dismiss it but still use some of its language in analysing their heroes' various strengths and weaknesses. Within some sports, e.g. tennis, golf, and athletics, its use is visible and expanding. In many other sports, e.g. rugby and football, much less use of it is made at this time.

One reason for this is the issue of individual versus team sport. To many people it is obvious how sports psychology can assist an individual, but much less clear how teams can use it. This is understandable but a misconception, and it is likely that more and more use will be made of sports psychology in team situations.

In Britain the increase in use will continue as the subject becomes more understood. This book, whilst not about psychology as such, broadly comes within this field. Readers who wish to explore the field of NLP further or to become specifically acquainted with sports psychology, can start this process by reading some of the books mentioned in the bibliography.

Chapter 2

A Brief Introduction To NLP

As stated already, this is not a book for the NLP expert. Its prime purpose is to help anyone interested in improving the levels of their sports performance. However, it is necessary to cover briefly some key aspects of NLP so that the reader can put these into context.

Richard Bandler and John Grinder, assisted by a number of people, (in particular Robert Dilts and Judith DeLozier) originated NLP in the United States in the early 1970s. It was based on modelling people who were highly effective in their fields and establishing how they did what they did (even if the person in question did not seem to know what it was they were actually doing, i.e. they were doing it naturally or unconsciously).

The original definition of NLP was 'the study of the structure of subjective experience', which is a wonderful description but can create mayhem in the minds of newcomers. It is not based upon some complex theory that needs to be analysed to be understood. In their book *Neuro-Linguistic Programming: Volume I The Study Of The Structure Of Subjective Experience* the originators make the point that

> *...it makes no commitment to theory, but rather has the status of a model – a set of procedures whose usefulness not truthfulness is the measure of its worth. NLP presents specific tools, which can be applied effectively in any human interaction. It offers specific techniques by which a practitioner may usefully organise and reorganise his or her subjective experience or the experience of a client* ***in order to define and subsequently secure any behavioural outcome.*** (My emphasis)

This can seem confusing to someone new to the field. Put simply, it means that we each have a model of the world based upon our values, beliefs, behaviour, experience, etc. However, everybody's model of the world is different. No two people are exactly the same in all respects. The reason is that the experiences we have are different, and our responses to experiences are different. Even people who have shared the same experience, e.g. a holiday, will view and remember it differently. A piece of music or a picture can create entirely different feelings, moods, emotions or reactions in different people. This is due to our individual responses to them.

Some people find this confusing, or even distressing, as they would prefer a world where everyone is the same and everything is predictable. Fortunately, NLP has shown us what most of us know already: that our capacity to be individual and unique is never-ending. NLP has given us a structure and a language to explain this.

This brings us back to part of the quote from the original Bandler, Grinder, Dilts and DeLozier book, the issue of what is *true*. We all believe we know the truth when we experience it. And, of course, we are right. It is just that it is *our* version of the truth!

Sport is a wonderful example of this. As anyone who watches sports events knows, opposing fans will see the game completely differently. Each person is seeing the same thing yet *living a different experience*. This is not just an issue of opposing fans having different opinions. Fans of the same team will debate and argue endlessly the merits of individual players' performance, re-run incidents that occurred. Newspaper columnists may then describe what appears to be a different game. Someone who saw the game on TV may describe something totally different.

This becomes even more pointed if you hear the players and managers discussing key incidents afterwards. In football a penalty incident is seen and described completely differently. In cricket an umpiring decision is debated from a large range of angles. How is it that everyone knows the truth? Often the more uncertain the options are, the more certain people are of their version, based upon their own model of the world. Rather than create an esoteric debate on the nature of truth, Bandler and Grinder took the view that it was the usefulness of something, not the perfect definition of truth, that was important. Instead of getting lost in the philosophical labyrinth, they concentrated on the question: does it work?

Building on this, they focused on the ecological aspects of what works. It is not sufficient to ruthlessly pursue a narrow, selfish ambition at the expense of other people, or even at the expense of our own peace of mind. Ecology in NLP is about making sure that what we do does not harm us or the people around us.

An individual who works on a mental aspect of performance that allows him/her to inflict unnecessary physical damage on an opponent would not be acting in an ethical or ecological way. This is an important issue, as it encourages us to improve our own performance without being 'untrue' to ourselves. NLP is not about a selfish search for success at the expense of personal happiness or causing damage to others. It is about achieving higher levels of performance and satisfaction whilst still being entirely true to oneself and, where appropriate, others as well.

The early work of Bandler, Grinder and the other originators provoked immense reaction at the time. As they had tended to model experts in communication, e.g. therapy, hypnosis and counselling, it was people from these fields who responded first. Many were sceptical, as they felt that the quick and permanent results that NLP achieved were a 'quick fix'. They believed that, because they had had to study for many years to achieve academic success and recognition in their field, their whole ethos was being threatened.

Others jumped onto the bandwagon and became NLP 'junkies', avidly attending training courses, and hungry for the next new technique they could try. Even now, some NLP courses have a quota of these people attending them. One other factor regarding the early history of NLP was that it originated in California and therefore the reaction of non-Americans meant that a certain scepticism prevailed.

Gradually through the seventies and eighties NLP developed greater use in wider fields. Part of the reason for this was that people who tried it found that it worked. This, along with the expansion of its use, particularly into business and sport, meant that more and more people heard about it, tried it, found that it worked and told others about it. Courses in NLP were created to reflect various levels of experience in the subject. Normally certification was awarded at the end of the course. Levels of certification were created that people could be trained to run. At the highest level this meant being qualified to train and certificate others, so that the message could be spread even further.

Part of its attraction, to many people, was that NLP did not ally itself to any one discipline. NLP took what worked from all sorts of fields – including psychology, philosophy, counselling, therapy, brain research, hypnotism and psychotherapy – and welded them together. Thus attendance at any NLP training normally involves mingling with a huge range of people from a wide variety of backgrounds.

Across the world various control bodies were established to monitor standards and promote NLP on as wide a front as possible. Increasingly, as the years have gone by, more and more books have been written on NLP. Particularly as the field has widened, some people have focused on specific aspects and turned them into specialist areas of their own. At this point NLP as an entity is known more widely than ever before, and the number of people who are exposed to it grows exponentially each year. In a very short time there will be virtually nobody who has not heard of NLP!

In business and sport many people are already using NLP techniques, without ever having heard of NLP itself. They have found something useful that they can use easily with very quick results, with no need to understand the concepts and jargon of NLP.

Over recent years specific developments in NLP have included its relationship with the Meyers Briggs Type Indicator, problem-solving, interpersonal skills training, leadership, establishing how some genius did what they did, probing how people use time in their lives, self-development, learning strategies and influencing skills.

The prospect of attending a 22-day practitioner certification, probably over a series of weekends, may not appeal to many people, but short, sharp sessions or easy to follow books will increasingly bring awareness of NLP to more and more people.

For those seeking qualification, one particular trend is to follow a distance-learning process using tapes and manuals. At present this represents a very small part of NLP training but a part which seems likely to grow steadily. The advent of accelerated learning techniques is also likely to impact on how people are trained in NLP. However, because NLP is such a practical subject, the actual 'doing of it' will always remain the key element in any certified training.

Outside the formal aspects of achieving a certified qualification, there is an increasing number of short, focused courses on specific aspects of NLP. These normally take up to three days and are highly intensive, great fun and can be put to use immediately. Normally it is not necessary to have any qualifications in NLP in order to attend these short courses.

The number of books now available is also growing at a dramatic rate. Most bookshops carry a range of NLP books, normally under the psychology section but increasingly in a section designated specifically to NLP. Increasingly most of the books are easy to understand, and it is normally best to buy one that has been recommended, try it, and then buy other books by the same author, or dip into the bibliography to follow a topic that seems interesting. The publishers of this book specialise in NLP and carry a wide range of titles.

For those new to NLP, some techniques will already be familiar, though you may not be aware that they originate from NLP.

Many of the techniques covered in this book overlap each other. This is quite deliberate. One of the fun ways for sportspeople to practise is to find a technique that works for them, then add in other ones that are allied, or appear to be relevant and worth a try. It is also fun to try something completely different, which may appear to make no sense and see what happens. Having fun is part of the spirit of NLP.

Chapter 3

Optimising Sports Performance Using NLP

You won't win if you come second.
Geoff Capes

In seeking to improve your individual performance it is necessary to be aware of a number of key points:

- Commit yourself to practising exercises and techniques over a period of time (a minimum of four weeks is suggested).
- Practise on a regular basis, daily if possible.
- Practise both physically and mentally.
- Work either on some specific aspect of your sport (e.g. improving confidence, winning when coming from behind), or choose a technique that seems to make sense and be fun to try.
- Don't choose too many aspects to work on too early. Rather practise one or two on a regular basis for a period and then widen out and try others.
- Suspend judgement by avoiding the trap of applying logic and intellectual judgement to a new technique. Rather, give it a try, create some early momentum, measure the results, then keep going. Remember these techniques are generative, i.e. the more you do them the more successful they become and the easier they get, as they become part of your repertoire of habits.
- Avoid telling yourself things like: 'I'm not really good enough' or 'This is too hard for me' or 'I can't understand this'. These become self-fulfilling prophesies, i.e. we make sure that they become true for us.
- Avoid putting yourself under too much pressure. These exercises and techniques should be fun!

- Consider working with someone else. This can often be done even in an individual sport. You don't have to be working on the same issue to work with someone else. Working in pairs or groups can significantly improve motivation and provide the impetus for trying things out.
- Apply a technique that works for you to more than one specific skill. Visualisation and anchoring, for example, can be applied to numerous aspects of improving sports performance. It isn't necessary to find a different technique for every issue.
- Choose an issue/skill to work on that is important to you rather than a low-key peripheral one.
- Experiment with trying different things. Avoid the trap of finding one thing that works and then relying only upon it. Try new things and enjoy having a go.

Section Two

Getting Ready

Chapter 4

Warm Up Mentally

Nowadays, even at a fun level, most people playing sport will warm up beforehand. This may take the form of a reasonably sophisticated approach or just comprise a few knee bends or stretching exercises. Even those who do not actually do any warming up know they should, such is the level of information around regarding the benefit of carrying out the process. Some will even go so far as to carry out a warm-down, a recent development for the occasional sportsperson, but seen as increasingly important by the professionals. When Bob Dwyer was rugby coach at Leicester Tigers the team became noted for carrying out , win or lose, an elaborate warm-down process immediately after the game.

The benefit of the physical warm-up is well known. Getting the body ready and adjusted for what is to come is essential to ensure that a high level of performance is achieved from the start. The reduction in injuries if an effective warm-up takes place is also obviously an important factor.

Many of the same benefits apply for mental warming up. In an individual sport it is vital that you are focused, ready to give your best right from the start, knowing what it is that you are trying to achieve. If there is a particular aspect of the game you are working on, attention needs to be paid to how you plan your campaign. Many sportspeople talk about 'getting their head right' before competing. Equally, sportspeople will often comment, after losing a game or contest they feel they should have won, that they just weren't there today, or that they could not focus or concentrate or that they kept letting other issues and thoughts pop into their mind.

Sally Gunnell talks of giving off positive vibes and pushing down the negatives. She also makes use of affirmations in her mental warming up. She was so focused and ready when she won the World Championships in 1993 that she didn't know she had won because she was so tunnel-visioned. This only happened twice in her career and is a product of being both physically and mentally warmed up and focused.

Source: *Equinox* TV Programme.

In team sports it is equally vital that mental warming up takes place. If one person in a team is not as prepared as the others this can affect the overall team performance. Worse, it can create friction within the team that in turn can cause long-term issues of bad feeling.

Another aspect of mental warming up relates to your opponent(s). At all levels of sport you could be playing against someone who knows your performance. Therefore they will have a clear idea of what they consider to be your strengths and weaknesses. They may well then play on your weaknesses – either physical or mental – in order to achieve victory. The worrying part of this is that it can then further embed limiting beliefs about your own abilities. For example, if an opponent believes you to be a slow starter, they may well set out to dominate you at the beginning. Equally if they believe you tend to crumble under pressure in a close game, they will have all sorts of ways to create and develop that pressure.

There is a fundamental difference between mental warming up and getting psyched up (which is covered in chapter 5). Mental warming up is a considered process, which is carried out on a regular, patterned basis to create the right frame of mind and for focusing on what is important.

In fact, some sportspeople seem to have a form of 'mental thermostat'. They have a preconceived idea of their own ability or level of performance, to which they then adhere. Sometimes they find themselves performing beyond their normal level, e.g. being ahead of a so called 'better' opponent, or playing a really good few holes at golf. Then, suddenly, the 'mental thermostat' kicks in and their performance reverts to its normal level. Repeated a few times this becomes evidence that their view of their ability was right all along – a 'self-fulfilling prophecy'.

It is vital to be clear about what it is that you're trying to achieve so that you can select the best approach. For example, one approach may be necessary to work on lack of confidence, while another is needed to focus on a specific technical aspect of the sport. Practice and willingness to 'mix and match' will help you to find which particular techniques are most useful and which are best used as part of mental warming up.

Captured within the phrase 'mental warm-up' are a whole host of terms. Some that you may have heard of are: visualising, mental rehearsal, cognitive rehearsal, correct practice and having a winning self-direction.

The key to the mental warm-up process is the ability to visualise or create images. One of the key points of NLP is that human beings process information through their five senses: visual, auditory, kinaesthetic (touch, feeling, and sensations) olfactory (smell) and gustatory (taste). In NLP these are called representation systems.

The visual system tends to be the most dominant representative system, although most sportspeople use all five senses to varying degrees. For example, the ability to see in the mind's eye the holiday resort we visited last year, and the front of the house we live in when we try to remember it, are types of visualising. Many people say that they cannot visualise, but if asked to remember one of the examples above they can do so immediately. Types of questions to ask so-called non-visual people are, 'What was the colour of your first car?' or, 'How many windows were there in the lounge of the house you were brought up in?' They will then, through the use of visualisation, be able to answer the question.

Some sportspeople expect their visualisation to look like a practice test card on a TV screen (and for some people it can do). However, normally it consists of a number of pictures appearing in our heads and we can choose to bring these images to the forefront of our attention. For some people this may take a little bit of practice, but most can achieve it very easily. This then allows for pre-play of a match beforehand and then replay afterwards, both very useful for the sportsperson.

The focus on the visual aspects of mental warm-up should not detract from the other four senses that we have. In many sports, e.g. cricket, tennis and squash, there is a particular sound which conveys an important piece of information to the brain that the sporting act has been carried out effectively. For example, in cricket there is a distinct and unique sound when the ball has been timed and hit correctly. This information is actually stored in the brain and is an important part of developing the skill of mentally warming up.

Also in many sports, e.g. shooting, golf and badminton where holding a piece of equipment is required, the feel of holding of the rifle, club or racquet correctly is evident to the sportsperson. Swimmers also will talk about 'being right in the water' because this is something they are able to recognise. Greg Louganis, the Olympic Champion diver, talked about hitting the board in the right spot and knew how this felt. Therefore his mental warm-up involved the appropriate kinaesthetic sense.

In order for it to be really useful it will require, for example, the tennis player to be able to see themselves hitting the ball properly, hear the sound that goes with it, recognise the feeling in the arm and body as the ball is hit. It might even mean smelling a particular smell that is unique to the court about to be played on, or tasting the sweet taste of victory rather than the bitter taste of defeat.

It is important to point out that mental warm-ups are not intended to be a substitute for physical preparation. The two are complementary and, used together, will increase levels of performance. However, to quote Richard H. Cox in his book ***Sports Psychology: Concepts And Applications*** 'mental practice by itself is more effective than no practice, and in certain circumstances is as effective as actual practice'.

An interesting point is that there is evidence available (Clark 1960) that the higher the level of performer, the greater the potential benefit in using visualising and mental warm-up. One reason for this is that the higher-level performer has already put in a higher amount of physical preparation and practice, has learned new physical techniques thoroughly, and has eliminated bad habits.

Mental techniques then provide the difference that makes the difference. This research has been available for many years but is only now being given greater attention.

Two final points before moving into some specific exercises. The ability to visualise used in this section as part of mental warm- ups is a very effective skill to be used in many areas of sport preparation and practice. It is very helpful, for example, in practising relaxation techniques and reducing stress, and, like many of the NLP techniques, is a generative process. Therefore its effects will increasingly become more powerful and easier to create.

Normally, physical preparation and practice take place at a specialist area away from the arena where the actual event will take place. If you have played at the arena before, or can get to see it prior to the event, you can build this into your mental warm-up by creating an appropriate picture of it in your preparation. However, you can still use mental warm-up exercises even if you are unfamiliar with the venue.

In preparing for the mental warm-up consider these factors:

- Your outcomes for the actual sporting event
- How you propose to achieve your outcomes
- How you feel about yourself, e.g. your physical preparation, awareness of your body and your thoughts, feelings and emotions about the event
- How you feel about the people around you
- How you feel about the team you belong to
- The actual place where the event will take place

Do these activities as part of your mental warm-up regime. It is designed to help you to experiment with your senses.

Activity

Establishing The Environment

- Find somewhere to sit comfortably. Don't lie downs, or you may fall asleep. Breathe deeply, slowly and regularly and close your eyes. Check that your body is relaxed all over, then start to play:

Activity

- Imagine yourself sitting on a beach looking at the sea. Notice the motion of the waves. Hear the sound of the waves lapping gently onto the beach. Feel the firmness and texture of the sand you are sitting on. Feel the heat from the sun as it gently touches your body.
- Recall the faces of loved ones. Hear the sound of their voices. Experience how they make you feel. Recall the smell and taste of them (if appropriate!).
- Remember the last meal you enjoyed. Go back and experience being there. Savour the taste of the food. Remember how it smelled. Replay the feelings as you ate it. Recall the people who were there. Hear the sound of their voices.
- Recall being under a shower. Feel the touch of the water. Feel the sensations of towelling down. Go through getting dressed mentally in sequence. Be aware of how each item of clothing feels.
- Remember a favourite piece of music. Experience how it makes you feel. See the picture it creates. Let your mind create whatever it wants.
- Remember a time when you performed particularly well, preferably in your sport, but it could be anything, e.g. a presentation at work, a joke that everyone laughed at, doing a job around the house. Revisit the best part. Use all five senses as appropriate.
- Explore and enjoy how you respond to this process.

This activity will get you used to knowing how it feels (and looks, sounds, smells and tastes) to play with your senses. The next activity is a specific NLP approach you can use to warm up mentally for any sporting event.

For it you will need to know the NLP terms 'association' and 'dissociation'. Association means being *inside* your own experience and body looking out from your own eyes. Dissociation means being outside your own experience and body, looking at yourself as if on a screen, having a sense of detachment and separateness.

The ability to move between being associated and dissociated is a very useful skill, which most of us do quite naturally. For example, practise reliving a variety of experiences, some of which are happy, some of which are sad. Test whether you are actually inside the experience, seeing it from your own eyes, (associated) or whether you are seeing yourself in the experience, as if watching it on a screen, or at least having a sense of being outside yourself (dissociated).

Many sportspeople use association and dissociation – either deliberately or unconsciously – in dealing with past events. For example, one way of handling a poor performance or a bad result is to review it in a dissociated state. Normally the emotions that attend the dissociated state are more detached, impersonal and easier to handle. This allows for a more reasoned analysis to take place.

Equally, the ability to be associated, i.e. fully inside and in tune with yourself, is vital for and effective for any sports (or other) performance. Being able to be fully aware of, and in control of, yourself at will, at the moment when peak performance is required, is a wonderful skill to have and to develop.

Mental Warming Up Activities

Activity

- Create an image of yourself performing all or a specific part of your sport to a very high standard. You need to do this in a dissociated state.
- Watch yourself carry out the sport, or the specific part of it you wish to develop. Get used to watching yourself, observing what you are doing well, having key points for attention.

- At a point that feels appropriate, step into the you that you are watching. Become fully associated, i.e. fully inside the you performing well. Become aware of everything that goes with performing well, e.g. how it looks, what sounds go with it, how it feels in terms of both your emotions and all your physical sensations. Feel the equipment that you are using. Experience the way the ground feels when you are in a state of perfect co-ordination and balance. It is a wonderful ability to be able to know and re-create performing well in a fully associated state. This then allows you to more regularly re-create high levels of achievement while actually performing.

Athlete's Awareness State Activity

- This is a technique often used by management trainers to create an expanded sense of awareness. It applies mainly to sports played within physical confines e.g. squash, snooker, and tennis, although it can be used to get used to a new or alien environment or 'away' changing room.
- Stand at one end of the court, pitch, room or hall and focus on a specific object or point at the far end. Give the object or point your total attention. Choose a point slightly above the eye line.
- Expand your sight and awareness to the two far opposite corners, noticing everything that this brings into vision. Do this without moving your head at all.
- Now expand your awareness down the walls, seats etc. towards yourself. Again, notice everything. Do this slowly.
- Take your expanded awareness behind you (without moving your head). Dwell on your senses, get used to how this state makes you feel.
- Repeat five or six times, as appropriate.

Like many NLP-based activities this may look strange written down. It may also seem time-consuming. Carried out 'live', however, it is actually very quick and easy to do, and the benefits, particularly in a new environment, are enormous.

Many sportspeople also apply mental warming up to the actual physical warming up process. In other words, they mentally practise the routine and rituals of the physical warming up, before the actual physical warming up takes place, and this forms part of their normal preparation process (For more on this, see chapter 19, ***Use Rituals And Habits***).

Chapter 5

Psych Up

When you are playing in front of the Kop, there is nothing else required to get psyched up.

Kevin Keegan

Although they are connected, there are important differences between mental warm-ups, psyching up and mental rehearsal, (mental warm-ups are discussed in chapter 4, while mental rehearsal is discussed in chapter 8).

Psyching up activities are used to raise the level of arousal and activity for a specific moment or event, e.g. rugby players prior to the start the game, or a weightlifter building up to a lift.

Another specific use for psyching up is in an individual or team situation where victory is apparently assured. Without psyching up, 'under psyching' may occur, in which the normal focus, adrenaline and attention are not evident and the individual or team struggles to perform at their normal level, or may actually lose.

It is important that someone who is a worrier, or who has low self-worth or lack of esteem, should not become too psyched up. It could result in their actually becoming so excited or aroused that their thinking could become blurred or distorted and they might turn into a 'headless chicken' or lose all notion of rationality and logic. In NLP terms this would then result in their developing a negative or non-resourceful 'programme'.

Utilised properly, psyching up is a vital part of the sportsperson's mental approach. Used indiscriminately, it will actually inhibit or reduce performance levels. Therefore it needs to be used with thought and caution.

Show me a man who is second, and I will show you a loser.

Stirling Moss

Activity

- Based upon previous performances you will know how you are and how you feel when you are fully ready to start, e.g. poised, confident, able to handle anything.
- Step into that state of preparedness, in a fully associated way. Notice exactly how it feels, both mentally and physically.
- Now capture that sensation in one word, image or feeling.
- In future, use that word, image or feeling whenever you need to feel fully psyched up.

Activity

- Practise the above psyching-up technique by carrying out a mental run-through of the game or part of it.
- Imagine yourself on the edge of losing.
- Then use your word, image or feeling to psych yourself up and turn the game around in your mind.

Activity

- Practice psyching up away from the sports arena, at home, in business, at leisure. The vital thing is to get your body and mind to know, recognise and be able to create their optimum psyching-up level at will. Don't be surprised if others notice your altered state as the signals are often very clear.

Chapter 6

Develop Positive Goals

To get going on the path to success, listen to Goethe. Whatever you can do, or dream you can, begin it.

Sir Ranulph Fiennes

Goal-setting and targeting have been long accepted as crucial aspects in improving sports performance. NLP has developed a simple but powerful model for setting and achieving them.

The sporting outcome process is:

Activity

- State your goal in the positive. A goal expressed as a negative, e.g. 'I don't want to fail' or 'I don't want to look stupid', is coded in the wrong language and will actually increase the likelihood of failure. Because of the way the mind works, it will have first to consider what is **not** required in order to get to what **is**. Although this seems obvious to many people, it is intriguing when talking to sportspeople how many find this step difficult.
- Your outcome must be under your control. Many people aim for a goal that is actually either partially or totally outside their sphere of influence or control. It is not enough to wish to get into the team if that outcome is influenced entirely by others. Much better to have a series of specific, performance-related outcomes, and which are under your control and you can do something about. The achievement of these outcomes will then actually put you in the position of moving towards or achieving a higher-level outcome. It also may well make this higher-level outcome become more within your level of control, and thus more achievable.

- Your outcome must be specific. Many sportspeople establish outcomes that are too vague, e.g. 'to be a better player', 'to achieve a higher level'. The outcome needs to be tangible and measurable, e.g. to get X per cent of your serves in first time, or to reduce your golf handicap to Y.
- Know what evidence there will be that your outcome has been achieved.
- Be very specific about this. If you achieve your time standard or win the game, what will you see (e.g. smiling faces), hear (e.g. applause, congratulations) and feel?
- The outcome must be ecological. In NLP this means that the outcome is an honourable and fair one, both to yourself and to others. To determine this, ask yourself these questions:
    - Does this particular goal fit in with all my other goals and with my family, work and friends?
    - Does it have honesty and integrity, and am I really committed?
    - Do I really want it?

This last question is important because you may decide that you don't really want to achieve your goal, once you have determined what its impact on your life may be, or how much work it will take. Remember that wishing alone will not get you what you want!

- Start right now. This sounds obvious, but it is fascinating how many sportspeople (and others!) say they want something to happen, but are not prepared to start. They prevaricate and procrastinate, always finding something else to do, or deciding to start tomorrow or next week. The percentage who start right now and see it through, in spite of occasionally slipping back, is a surprisingly small one.

Having dealt with the process of creating realistic outcomes, it is worth dwelling briefly on why they are so important. Research evidence shows that outcome-setting in sport works more often than it doesn't. One reason is that setting an outcome will make you more focused and productive, more willing to do what is necessary to achieve your outcome. Also, provided you have set the outcome yourself, you have greater commitment to achieving it.

This leads us to the distinction between outcome and performance orientation. In sports psychology terms, outcome-orientation is about winning or losing rather than how the outcome or result is achieved. Performance-orientation is based upon the **how,** i.e. the quality of the performance rather than the specific result. This might seem an odd distinction but it is an important one. Focusing solely on the result can have the effect that the means of achievement may get overlooked and therefore not improved for a future tougher opponent.

According to Locke, Shaw, Saari and Latham (1981), goals have four benefits:

- They create focused attention
- They create energy
- They create long-term willingness to keep going
- They create the opportunity for new learnings

They also help achieve what Stephen Covey calls 'response – ability,' i.e. the ability that all of us have to control our own responses.

> *I always had a target: get into the team, play every game, improve my fitness and levels of performance. Targets are the key to life.*
>
> Kevin Keegan

Chapter 7

Create Effective Preparation Strategies

Nowadays it seems almost unnecessary to point out that sportspeople should put as much energy – both physical and mental – into the preparation as into the actual event itself. However, it is only in recent years that the importance of preparation has become generally accepted. Even today some sportspeople still think that preparation requires only a physical warm-up and a bit of psyching up for good measure. Others, however, are very aware of the dangers of this narrow approach.

> *It is always easy to be focused and 'up' for the challenge when you are the underdogs, but the real art of professionalism comes from performing again and again when you are* ***expected*** *to succeed – that marks out the true champions.*
>
> Phil de Glanville

Terry Orlick shows the balance of key factors in an interesting way:

Performance	=	**Physical Preparation**	+	**Technical Skill**	+	**Psychological Readiness**

It may seem odd, but it is also necessary to create effective preparation strategies. In order to do this, start by asking yourself these questions:

a. What is my desired outcome for the preparation (see Chapter 6, ***Develop Positive Goals***)?
b. What does this outcome say about me as a sportsperson, my beliefs, strengths, weaknesses etc.?
c. How will I know that I have achieved my preparation outcome?
d. What specific techniques do I want to work on as part of my preparation, e.g. association/dissociation, anchoring etc?
e. Should I keep a written list of my outcomes and progress? If so, this list should be updated on a regular basis.
f. How will I reward myself when my preparation has achieved its outcome?

Activity

- Affirmations

  Use single words or a short sentence to get yourself ready to perform e.g. 'I am a winner' or 'success'!

Activity

- Focusing your attention

  In preparing effectively, wandering eyes mean a wandering mind, a mind that encourages interference factors to intrude. Focus your attention through visualising (thus focusing internally, inside your head), or by focusing on a particular object or person. Try to eliminate all other sights and sounds.

Activity

- Using distraction

  Instead of focusing nervous or negative attention on the upcoming game, try diverting and diffusing your attention by doing something else. Listen to relaxing music on headsets or do anything else that will take your mind off the game (when Dean Richards and Jeremy Guscott played rugby for England, they used to distract themselves by playing cards).

Activity

- Breaking down outcomes

  If the goal or outcome that you have set seems too large or difficult, break it down into more realistic and achievable chunks. This will help you to achieve some success more quickly and easily, and will motivate you to achieve further success.

Activity

- Relaxation

  Many great sportspeople have an amazing ability to 'switch off' just before an important event. Mohammed Ali could sleep just before a big fight, George Best before a game. In a different context Winston Churchill catnapped most afternoons, even at the height of the war. Sleep obviously worked for these people, but don't try it if you tend to wake up feeling irritable or worse than you felt before you slept. Relaxation does not necessarily require sleep. Indeed many relaxation exercises are designed to ensure that sleep does not occur. Chapter 25, ***Use Relaxation Techniques***, gives some examples of relaxation techniques.

Activity

- Studying the environment

  This means becoming familiar with the stadium, the field of play, the court, the course, etc. In addition, if playing away, it can be very helpful to familiarise yourself with the changing rooms, where you will sit and change, where the toilet facilities are. When David Steel made his debut for England at cricket at Lord's he had only ever played previously for his county and had therefore only ever played in the away dressing room. When his turn to bat came he got lost on his way out and found himself in the basement. With the cricketing world waiting for him he was nowhere to be seen! It says a great deal for his abilities that he did not allow this to upset or distract him from his purpose.

Activity

- Develop positive rituals and habits

  There is a difference between a ritual and a superstition. Used effectively, rituals and habits are a vital part of effective preparation. The NLP technique of anchoring (covered below) is one way of achieving this.

Overview on Anchoring

Anchoring is defined in NLP as the process by which we make associations between experiences, e.g. hearing a particular voice and feeling good, seeing a certain person and feeling grumpy. It is any association or trigger that evokes a response. The way that this works is that the brain makes these associations naturally and of its own accord. It is an entirely unconscious process that can be made conscious, built upon and utilised.

We all use anchoring (often unconsciously) to alter our state. For example, we may look at a set of holiday photographs to be reminded of pleasant memories. For many people the playing of sport itself is an anchor as it changes the state the person is in.

The other key point in anchoring is that as well as changing your state, it allows you to create a peak moment. This means drawing together – like a 'kettle coming to the boil' – all the resources you require at a particular moment in time. With skill and practice you can use the process of anchoring to create 'the zone' or 'white moment' that sportspeople are always searching for, at the moment when it is most required.

Activity

The steps in creating effective anchors are:

- Identify a resource state you want as a sportsperson e.g. concentration, confidence in a specific situation, the ability to relax and go with the flow.
- Recall a specific occasion in your life when you had that resource.
- Go back to that occasion, relive (access) the state, be totally aware of what you could see, hear, feel, smell and taste.
- Come back to the here and now and choose your anchors (triggers) to evoke the response you want. The anchor can be in whichever of the five senses (representation systems) is appropriate e.g. a specific image, a specific word or phrase, or clutching a part of the anatomy such as a finger, an ear lobe or part of the face. The more of the five senses that can be combined for the anchor the more powerful the anchor will be.
- In your mind's eye put yourself back fully into the resource state you want, e.g. concentration. Be aware of what you can see, hear, feel, smell and taste. Be fully in touch with all your senses. If there is a series of events involved, relive them in sequence. Adopt only associated body positions, or use any relevant kit or equipment.

- As the resourceful feeling is building up to its optimum point, connect up (fire) all your anchors: see your image, say your word or phrase, make your gesture or touch.
- Repeat the steps above five or six times to build all the connections thoroughly.
- Test the anchor. Put the image, word, feeling or gesture, smell or taste together. Notice how the anchor brings back the resourceful state. If this seems not to be working, go back and repeat the earlier steps as often as required.
- Test the anchor again.
- Mentally rehearse your anchors as part of your preparation and training.
- Use your anchors before and/or during the actual sporting event.

An actual example of effective anchoring is the squash player whose anchor consisted of seeing an image of himself on the T, using the word 'control' and putting his right hand to his left knee prior to the actual game starting. No one around him knew what he was doing, but he was able to build on the anchor game after game.

One of the constant themes of this book is the generative aspect of NLP techniques, i.e. the more you use them the easier and more powerful they become. This is particularly true of anchoring. In fact it is vital that anchors are used frequently both in preparation and during play. Using an anchor every few months may help to a certain extent, but not as much as it can if it is used more regularly.

You can have as many anchors for as many situations as you like. Anchors are also extremely useful when used either consciously or unconsciously by team-mates and/or coaches. In fact, sportspeople are surrounded by anchors. In Dean Richards' words 'The key moment was entering the arena, that's when it all came together and meant something'. This is an example of an anchor for him.

Another useful NLP technique for creating effective preparation strategies is to use association and dissociation. When you are associated, you are inside your own body, experiencing something through your own eyes. When you are dissociated, it is like you are outside your own body, observing yourself as if on a screen.

Activity

Normally experiences that are associated are more live and real. Dissociated experiences tend to be a little more detached, a bit like looking at some old photographs that don't mean very much any more. One way to establish which are which is to consider a range of the experiences from the past. Try thinking back over past events, both good and bad, recent and more distant.

For example:

- passing your driving test
- getting married
- failing an exam
- a good sports performance
- a bad sports performance
- a car accident
- a sexual encounter
- receiving good (or bad) news

As you think about each event, notice if you are associated or dissociated.

Most of you will find that you were associated in some experiences and dissociated in others.

What makes this useful is that we can actually choose whether to associate or dissociate i.e. we can choose our response to a situation. Therefore we can heighten a sports experience by associating to make it more real and powerful, or we can dissociate to lessen the impact. Again this is perfectly natural, and a lot of sportspeople deal with a defeat by dissociating from it. This may or may not always be a good thing, but it is an interesting choice to have. Other sportspeople may associate with a defeat and use it 'to beat themselves up' and further embed beliefs regarding their own abilities. The danger of this is that it can help create a self-fulfilling prophecy, e.g. 'I always knew I wasn't really good enough to win.'

The ability to dissociate is an important one, as it enables fear, stress and anxiety to be dealt with purposefully.

Activity

- Put yourself back into a situation in which you are strongly associated. Try becoming dissociated, i.e. watching yourself from the outside. Feel what this does to the experience, then switch back to being associated.
- Take a dissociated experience and put yourself inside it. See it from the inside through your own eyes, notice what this does to the experience, then switch back to being dissociated.
- Take a bad sporting experience that you now realise you associate with, and dissociate from it. Notice what this does to the experience, then leave the bad sporting experience as a dissociated one.

Chapter 8

Rehearse Mentally

Because the brain is not able to distinguish between a real event and one that has been highly intensely imagined, mental rehearsal plays a large part in improving sports performance. Almost every interview with a famous sportsperson carries some comment regarding the mental or psychological aspects of their game.

Sally Gunnell talks about mentally rehearsing a race, paying particular attention to being in the right position coming off the last bend. She then rehearses making the right moves to ensure that she finishes the race in first place. What is fascinating is how she discusses dealing with having weak thoughts and (still inside her head) seeing herself not making the right moves and therefore not winning the race. Should this start to occur, she doesn't allow the mental rehearsal to continue but immediately stops it, gets herself back together, re-focuses, then rehearses the race again in her head, this time ensuring that she does everything right and wins the race.

Source: *Equinox* TV Programme

Duncan Goodhew talks about swimming the race thousands of times in his mind. Knowing the perfect dive into the water (a major kinaesthetic experience), knowing the right number of strokes in the first length, executing the perfect turn, upping the stroke rate in the second length, even mentally rehearsing the perfect touch at the end.

Source: MAST Conference

Both Gunnell and Goodhew tell these stories without any mention of NLP, yet their strategies incorporate NLP techniques and can be explained in NLP terms.

One way to get used to mental rehearsal is to consider the way you are already doing it. This might seem a strange comment to make as many amateurs (and even some professionals) would deny that they do it. However, in preparing for, travelling to, getting changed for an event, a little voice might be saying, 'I don't feel so good today', or there may be a lack of ability to concentrate, or a too healthy respect for the opponent. Alternatively the voice could be saying 'Today is the day' or 'This is it and I'm ready'.

Be aware that negative voices and messages in your head are mentally rehearsing and pre-programming you for failure!

Activity

Work out the mental rehearsing that you currently do whether you do it consciously or not. Answering these questions will help.

In the time immediately **before** the event takes place:

- Do you feel focused, poised, confident, high in energy, in control, able to get it right without trying too hard?
- Do you feel relaxed, calm, tolerant, easy-going, ready to go with the flow, and see what happens?
- Do you feel tense, full of nervous energy, uncertain about your game plan or what is going to happen, easily distracted, likely to get irritated by something, burning unnecessary energy?
- Do you feel flat, lethargic, not really bothered, not in control, tired, not really ready for it?

If you are in the first state, you are much more likely to achieve success than if you are in the last of these states. In other words, the first state pre-programs you for likely success, while the last state pre-programs you for likely failure.

With NLP it is possible to change your pre-program by using mental rehearsal. One of the major advantages of mental rehearsal is that it can be drawn on at almost any time and doesn't require that you are in the actual venue or field of play. In fact, if you use NLP processes, you can carry the event with you inside your head. This is something you have probably been doing unconsciously, but NLP can help you do it consciously, where you have more control over it.

For the professional or experienced sportsperson there is one other vital factor to consider. Studies show that people at a more advanced level gain greater benefit from mental rehearsal than beginners. This is explained by the fact that at the early learning stages most beginners are going into thinking and sensory overload. There is so much to learn, and at that stage none of it has become natural or habitual. Also it may be difficult to mentally rehearse because the beginner does not know what a good performance looks, hears, feel, smells or tastes like.

The potential problem in this situation is that beginners may develop bad habits physically and mentally. Then, when they are ready to start using mental rehearsal they have already pre-programmed themselves into all sorts of disempowering beliefs. NLP can help, but naturally it is easier if such beliefs are not allowed to develop in the first place.

The professional or more experienced sportsperson, on the other hand, has made many parts of their game natural and habitual. They can then choose a smaller, more specific part of it to work on. They are also more likely to recognise the results achieved (although even at the highest levels many sportspeople are both physically and mentally rehearsing bad habits and technique).

All of this does not mean that amateurs or beginners cannot or should not use mental rehearsal. What it does mean is that mental rehearsal must be approached with thought and planning. Working on a developing strength, taking one skill at a time, giving a few minutes a day in the early stages, are all ways to help develop the right approach to mental rehearsal.

> *About two hours before kick off I will sit in a bath in my hotel room with the TV and radio switched off and the door closed and I will relax. It is here that I go through my final mental rehearsal and preparation for the game. I will go through in my mind the first tackle, the first catch, the first line-out, the first scrum and the role that I play in each of these. I will use positive events from the past to refer to, so that by the time I get out of the bath fifteen minutes later, my mind is totally focused and ready for the challenge.*
>
> Tim Rodber, *Mental And Physical Fitness For Sport* (1996) Hodder & Stoughton

Mentally rehearsing a perfect performance is essential. However, it is just as important to rehearse strategies for when things may not be going perfectly.

Greg Louganis, the American Olympic diving champion, talks about there being a sweet spot on a diving board. When the sweet spot is hit the chances of the dive being correct are substantially improved. But what happens when the sweet spot isn't hit? He cannot pull out of the dive. It is vital to be able to respond and produce the perfect dive, even though the sweet spot wasn't hit in the first place.

Source: AND – *Train The Trainers* Tape

It is possible to develop a list of specific skills, abilities and responses that you want to work on, in order to be able to handle any situation that may occur.

Before going on to describe some activities to be practised in developing mental rehearsal skills, here is a short case-study of how NLP techniques were used (in a fairly unusual way) to help a young squash player.

> *Andy was thirteen years old, well coached and extremely good for his age. The difficulty that he had was in the back corner on the backhand side where he had difficulty getting the ball back, except in a defensive way.*
> *Having played a lot of squash he knew what the ball should sound like as it came off the racket having been hit correctly. Rather than get him to physically practise, with the risk of*

de-motivating him and perhaps embedding a bad habit, it was decided to try something different.

He was asked to rehearse, in his mind's eye, seeing, feeling, and in particular hearing the ball coming off the racket properly when played from the back corner. For a thirteen-year-old this could have seemed an unusual request, but he was willing to give it a try.

Over a period of a month he did no physical practice on that particular aspect of his game. Instead he rehearsed the shot mentally six times in a block, repeated six times a day. Because of the speed of squash this only took a few minutes each time.

When, after the month was over, he started to practise again, the results were astonishing. Not only could he play the shot in a more attacking manner on a consistent basis, his feet, shoulders, body were all moving in the right way to allow the shot to be played. Working the other way round, i.e. getting him physically to move his feet etc. in the right way may well have worked but it could have taken much longer with lots of problems along the way.

The other benefit of the story is of course that Andy could see measurable, tangible, improvements in his game and therefore was eager to use mental rehearsal in all other parts of his squash.

These activities are intended to provide an introduction to mental rehearsal. The process is fairly simple, and you can make up your own, or work with team-mates or your coach.

Activity

- Get into a relaxed physical and mental state.
- Choose the skill or ability to work on.
- Allow your mind to gather as much information as is required about the event, e.g. the court, course, pitch, venue, crowd, timing, opposition, etc.
- Notice what you seem to be paying close attention to, then note any other significant factors.
- If appropriate, run through the build-up to the event, putting your kit on, checking your equipment, etc. (see chapter 19, ***Use Rituals And Habits***)
- Run through in your mind's eye the performance as you want it be, be fully associated (inside) the experience – unless you have deliberately decided to be dissociated from (outside) it.
- If any aspect of the performance is not running smoothly, either stop and change it, or see yourself dealing purposefully with it.
- Break state (think/do something else for a few seconds) then run the mental rehearsal again.

After carrying out the process it is very useful to review it by asking:

- Which of my five senses (seeing, hearing, feeling, tasting, smelling,) were the most important?
- Were any of my senses more difficult to rehearse?
- What impact did my five senses have on my mental rehearsal?

Because of NLP's generative power, it can help you to build on previous successes – both mental and physical – to improve your performance further and further.

Chapter 9

Develop Self-confidence

Use everything to develop your self-confidence.
Kevin Keegan

Self-confidence is an important issue for both amateurs and professionals. Professionals are much more likely to have, and display, a greater sense of confidence in their skills and abilities. But this may not apply to every aspect of their sport. In other words, even at professional level, there may well be some aspect of the game where the player is not totally confident.

An example of this is where a professional, high-performance club player is picked to play internationally for the first time. Some seem born to it. Others (sometimes even the most naturally talented) struggle and never quite establish themselves. The difference more often than not isn't just ability. After all, people do not get to international level without the necessary ability. It is much more about what happens inside their head, what they actually think about themselves, and sometimes what they think about their team-mates and opponents.

Lee Chapman, the ex-footballer, talks about losing confidence when playing at Arsenal. When he moved to Leeds he became the League's top scorer. 'Time stood still, the goal was very large, there was no thought of failure'.

Source: *Equinox* TV Programme

Activity

The questions covered in the mental rehearsal section regarding how sportspeople feel before an event are worth repeating here:

- Do you feel focused, poised, confident, high in energy, in control, able to get it right without trying too hard?
- Do you feel relaxed, calm, tolerant, easy-going, ready to go with the flow and see what happens?
- Do you feel tense, full of nervous energy, uncertain about your game plan or what is going to happen, easily distracted, likely to get irritated by something, burning unnecessary energy?
- Do you feel flat, lethargic, not really bothered, not in control, tired, not really ready for it?

Carrying these states onto the field of play will affect your sports performance. Some sportspeople find that once they are on the actual field everything comes right. Others find that they cannot shake off their negative state and their performance is affected.

Another factor that can impact on developing confidence is what psychologists call 'learned helplessness'. In essence this means that sportspeople may avoid doing something because they have failed in the past, or because they do not believe that they can succeed. This leads to embedded levels of poor confidence and performance which may ultimately lead to depression.

Activity

Some of the questions regarding self-confidence for all sportspeople are:

- Do I feel true self-confidence deep inside, or is it just a front?
- Do I share my confidence in order to help others?
- Do I have a realistic self-image, i.e. do I know myself well?
- Do I make things happen, or do I wait for them to happen?
- Do I know my goals, achieve them, upgrade them, and enhance my sense of self-worth through them?
- Do I see things through to the end?
- Do I notice what other self-confident people do?

Within sports psychology there are a number of models of self-confidence. For those who wish to pursue these further, the best-known ones are Bandura's theory of self-efficacy, Harter's competence-motivation theories, Nicholls' developmentally-based theory of perceived ability and Vealey's sport-specific model of sport confidence. All of these are explained in *Sports Psychology, Concept And Applications* by Richard Cox. The two threads that run through the research are that realistic self-expectation and confidence are vital for achieving high levels of sports performance, and that helping young children to develop self-confidence is highly effective in achieving satisfaction and success in their sport.

Another key factor in developing self-confidence is the issue of how failure is dealt with. Everyone, at all levels of sport, knows someone who is never wrong: their equipment lets them down, the referee was against them, or their opponent just got lucky. In addition to avoiding responsibility for their own performance, this allows them to retain their self-image and confidence about how good they believe they are. The thought pattern is, "I'm as good as I thought I was, but due to factor A, B, C, etc. it didn't happen." This of course may be partially true, but it is unlikely to be as true as they believe it to be. Truly self-confident sportspeople are aware of factors over which they have no control, but they also take responsibility for their own performance.

All great sportspeople (at whatever level they play) have had to start from somewhere. Very few have always and consistently been great. Building on success is obviously a key factor that is also about having a deep inner confidence in yourself. One way which NLP can help this, for example, is by using the anchoring process. It is also possible to take the confidence that you have experienced in one activity, e.g. playing the piano, giving a speech, and build it into improving your sports performance.

To some people this seems odd. You may believe that you lack confidence in everything that you do. However, there may be certain activities, such as sewing, gardening, driving the car, or working out figures, where you are obviously competent, relaxed and confident. You may say, 'Oh that, that doesn't count, it's not important.' Try telling that to someone who would love to be able to do one of those skills! Very few people lack confidence in *every* aspect of their lives. NLP allows us to find it in one area and apply it in other areas.

NLP also gives us the techniques to model someone else being confident in a sporting situation and to use that to help improve our own performance. Therefore lack (or loss) of confidence does not have to be the problem that many people believe it is. It is possible to see every situation, even when something doesn't work, as an opportunity to develop confidence. This is not just the self-hype it might appear. There are very few situations where it is not possible to find something specific and tangible that can be built on.

It is important to concentrate on developing self-confidence during training, using physical training as an opportunity to develop the mental side as well. For most sportspeople having worked hard in training, both physically and mentally, reaps its own reward.

The good news is that the majority of the NLP techniques covered in this book can be applied to developing self-confidence. In particular the anchoring and submodality activities covered in chapter 7 are enormously powerful in this regard.

Activity

Richard J Butler, in his book *Sports Psychology In Action* describes an exercise he titles 'a positive frame of mind'. This exercise involves describing three aspects of yourself as a sportsperson, bearing in mind that your description must:

- be stated positively.
- be in your own words.
- refer to behaviours that you can control.

Thus while 'age' might be considered to give you an edge, it is not within your control. Think specifically what it is about your age which gives you the edge, e.g. enthusiasm, speed, single-mindedness.

- It is better to refer to specific events or behaviours rather than global terms like 'personality'. A similar question concerning what it is about your personality, e.g. thoughtful, courageous, assertive, would provide more specific and controllable descriptions.

Write down your descriptions of those three aspects of yourself under these headings:

- strengths
- improvements
- achievements
- preparation
- edge
- previous performance

Use this information to help you to set an outcome for the next time you play or compete.

Activity

The NLP technique known as the swish pattern is very powerful in building self-confidence.

- Identify a sporting situation where it would be useful to feel more confident.
- Create a detailed picture of this situation in your mind.
- Now create a second picture of the situation, seeing yourself behaving as if you are self-confident. Make changes to the picture until it is absolutely right. Do this in a dissociated state.
- Make the first picture (the negative one, where you lack confidence) as big and bright as possible. Place a smaller, darker image of the second picture (the positive one, where you are confident), in the bottom right hand corner of the negative picture.
- Make the second (positive) picture grow bigger and brighter, covering the first (negative) picture so that the negative picture grows dim and shrinks away. Do this as quickly as you can say 'swish'. The faster this happens the better.
- Repeat the last step at least five times, repeating the word 'swish' on each occasion.
- Now you can either:
  - do a future pace (see chapter 28, ***Deal With Difficulties***)
  - try to recreate the first picture. If the swish has worked this will be difficult, because it will look and feel different. If the picture is the same, repeat the steps.
- Imagine the situation once again. If you see yourself repeating the old behaviour, go through the steps again.

Activity

Another useful activity is called the Circle of Excellence.

- Imagine an invisible circle on the floor. Make it three feet in diameter and two feet in front of you.
- Now think back to a time when you were on top of everything, when you were successful and everything you did worked. If you cannot remember such a time and make one up, imagine it fully. Alternatively base it on a TV or film star – it doesn't matter as long as you evoke a strong state.
- In a dissociated state examine all your five senses. See yourself inside the circle excelling. Imagine what the 'you' inside the circle is seeing, hearing, feeling, smelling, tasting.
- Step into the circle and become fully associated. Notice what you are seeing, hearing, feeling, smelling and tasting. Anchor this kinaesthetically so that you have the resource always available.

This activity is specifically designed to bridge the gap between ability and true confidence.

Activity

Use affirmations based on the five senses. Do this by completing the sentence:

I know I am performing well because

- I (whatever you see)
- I (whatever you hear)
- I (whatever you feel, including sensations, muscles, tactile responses)
- I (whatever you taste)
- I (whatever you smell)

Now complete this sentence, following the same pattern: I am confident because I make a habit of thinking, talking and acting in a confident way. I know this because...

Section Three

Building And Improving

Chapter 10

Create A Successful Approach

A theme that has run through this book is the issue of how much of the sportsperson's mental approach is pre-set and how much can be developed or changed. Many people believe that we are pre-formed, set in tablets of stone, and that nothing can be changed. Others believe that change may be possible, but that people should not be 'tampered with'. Some sportspeople also worry about analysing their performance too much, in case, by analysing it, they will somehow destroy it.

There is no doubt that, as in all walks of life, there are exceptional people. No one would deny the genius of a Jeremy Guscott, a David Gower, or a Michael Owen. However, for every one of these there are hundreds of other mere mortals who are still able to play to a good level. It is possible for all of us to develop the approaches necessary to enjoy the sport, compete to a level and develop improved skills.

The statement is often made that the naturals 'just have it', as if by magic. And of course they do. The question is what can the rest of us do to develop ourselves. It may not be possible to actually become Jeremy Guscott, but it is possible to become your own version of him. In other words, it is possible to model some aspects of what he does and build them into your own approach. In talking to successful people in all walks of life, including sportspeople, it is fascinating to hear how they think about themselves, their approach to their sport and their opponents.

When it comes to establishing what makes sportspeople 'tick', why they do what they do, or what makes some sportspeople different, the first place to check is their Meta Programs. These are filters, or ways of seeing the world, that help explain why people do (or do not do) certain things. When we become aware of our Meta Programs, we are able to alter them.

In sport, as in all walks of life, the amount of information that the brain needs to absorb and make sense of is enormous. Most information is absorbed unconsciously. It is simply not possible, for example, for a footballer to take in every piece of information regarding his own physiology and mental state as well as the pitch, the opposing team, the referee, the crowd etc. on a conscious level. Most of this information is absorbed unconsciously, and the way we absorb it depends upon the Meta Programs that we use. Eleven Meta Programs are described here:

10.1 Moving Towards Or Moving Away

I always have targets to work to, you have to be moving toward something.

Kevin Keegan

In discussions with sportspeople it is intriguing to ask them what their approach is to training. Many of them even at a professional level will say that they *must* attend training because otherwise there will be some negative consequence, e.g. not being fit enough, or not being considered for the team. Their language indicates that the key driver is a fear of negative consequences rather than something enjoyable, rewarding, fun and pleasurable. They are *moving away* from something negative.

On the other hand, sportspeople who look forward to training, and want to do it in order to improve their fitness or performance so that they can reach their goals, are moving towards something positive.

As with all the Meta Programs there are ways of establishing which pattern is being used. Most of these indicators are linguistic and can be heard in everyday conversation. Listen to the words you use in conversations with others, and listen to your own internal dialogue. In reality you may not be wholly moving towards or away in a specific context, and may be somewhere in between. Therefore with each Meta Program there are a range of options. For moving towards or away these are:

- moving towards
- moving towards with some moving away
- equally balanced between moving towards and away
- moving away with some moving towards
- moving away

A similar pattern applies with all the Meta Programs.

In addition the issue of the context or situation cannot be over-emphasised. You may use the moving towards pattern in some contexts, and the moving away patterns in others. Some examples of contexts for the sportsperson are:

- training
- mental preparation
- warming up
- early parts of the performance
- middle parts of the performance
- towards the end of the performance
- when things are difficult
- when things are easy
- playing below form
- over- or underestimating the opponent
- dealing with a crowd
- analysing the performance afterwards

Profile: Moving-towards Sportspeople

These sportspeople focus on what they do want – not on what they don't. They focus on the future, work to positive goals, and are open to changes in routines providing there is clear purpose.

How to recognise them:

- they focus on progress, moving forward
- their language (or internal dialogue) includes expressions like, 'let's go for it', 'let's get going', 'we're making progress'
- they tend to be active, quick to try new things, open to ideas, and often include other people in what is going on
- they have positive goals, i.e. they will play to improve

a skill or level of performance rather than simply to survive or get through

In coaching them :

- use positive incentives, rather than threats
- remove blockages to skill and performance progress, rather than concentrating on the problem areas
- view failure as useful feedback that will help in moving forward
- focus on what is working well just as much as you focus on what is not working
- use positive goals
- plan for improving performance

Profile: Moving-away Sportspeople

These sportspeople tend to focus on what is wrong, difficult or not working. They will often find reasons not to stretch themselves or work towards new goals. They tend to over-analyse performance problems instead of seeking new forward-based solutions.

How to recognise them:

- they tend to be fatalistic about what happens to them, as though it is beyond their control
- they use language or internal dialogue about what is not going well, problem areas that might go wrong, or how to avoid things
- their language is often passive rather than active
- they tend to look for the flaws in a situation
- they frequently use words and phrases like *can't, won't, hard, tough, not getting anywhere, won't work*

In coaching or supporting them:

- establish clear positive goals
- focus on improvements in performance
- start using language and internal dialogue that matches theirs
- clarify what might go wrong, where it will be tough, then establish clear objectives

Based on the above it can sound as though moving towards is good and moving away from bad. This is not necessarily the case. Many people have achieved a great deal by moving away from. For example, many sportspeople, particularly boxers, have achieved great success by moving away from poverty, others have achieved success by moving away from a club or an area. So it is simplistic to say that moving away from is worse or less effective than moving towards. Also, everyone – no matter how successful a sportsperson they might be – has some context in which they are moving away from.

The issue becomes more important when considering goals and feeling happy with levels of achievement. Sportspeople who move towards know when they have achieved a particular goal and then establish another appropriate one. Sportspeople who move away from tend to focus on when they are in trouble rather than on having a level of achievement or satisfaction that they are working towards. The drive to not be in a situation, or to know what they don't want rather than what they do, can mean that they can be unnecessarily hard on themselves or make improving performance harder than it needs to be. This can result in mixed levels of self-esteem and a blaming of various circumstances for so called 'failure'.

Another issue is maintaining a consistent approach. One of the phenomena of successful sportspeople and sports teams is what happens when they achieve their original level of success or objective. Many sportspeople, in all sports, 'go off the boil' when the original objective is achieved, i.e. winning a certain tournament or competition, or becoming established in the team. One reason for this is that they have achieved their original moving towards objective and have not yet established another goal to move towards.

In fact many of them, whether in individual or team sports, change from a moving towards objective to a moving away, i.e. maintenance of a level of performance, not losing, playing safe, coasting. At this point their performance tends to lose its original impetus. The individuals or teams, like Steve Redgrave or Manchester United, that are able to achieve a consistently high level of performance year in and year out, seem to be the exception rather than the rule.

10.2 Options Or Procedures

This second Meta Program pattern has to do with the reasons that sportspeople have for their actions, based upon the amount of choices they have. Are they seeking new ways to approach training and the game, or are they happy to stick to the tried and trusted ways they have used before?

Profile: Options Sportspeople

These are sportspeople who look for new ways to approach training or the game. They may take risks with something new in their quest for a better way. They are motivated by new ideas and will try new things even when tried and trusted routines have worked well previously. No matter how successful something has been in the past they will look for a different (and hopefully better) way.

How to recognise them:

- they look for new ways to approach situations
- they like to have lots of choices
- they become bored and lose interest quickly if things become routine
- they tend to use words like *new, try, challenge, interesting,* when describing their approach or why they did something
- they see the potential in new ideas or new ways of doing things
- they tend to be future-oriented
- they continually challenge the status quo

In coaching or supporting them:

- get them to see how new ideas can be used
- allow them some freedom (with appropriate parameters if appropriate) to change things or be spontaneous

- ask them for new ideas
- use words such as *alternatives, possibilities, choice, new, different*

Profile: Procedures Sportspeople

These are sportspeople who like the tried, the tested and the trusted. Their attitude is: 'If it ain't broke don't fix it'. This is based on their view that there is a best or right way. They are not interested in choice, new ways or changing things for change's sake. They believe that things started should be seen through right to the end.

How to recognise them:

- they tend to be factual in describing a sporting experience, explaining the background and development of a situation and how it came to be
- they will explain a set of circumstances by explaining how something came to happen, saying that they did not really choose it
- they tend to sit back in training sessions and meetings, waiting for something to happen
- they tend not to reveal much emotion in their body-language
- if a procedure is changed or violated they will want to go through it and analyse it thoroughly
- they tend to be upset by too many changes or new things happening at the same time

In coaching or supporting them:

- make them aware of the end purpose in what they are doing
- when dealing with something new ensure that everything is fully explained
- show them that you have respect for them and their views and approach
- use words and phrases such as *correct, known, understood, tested, proven, the right way*

The coach, manager or player who is strongly procedural will consider the options person to be a maverick. The options manager, coach or player will consider the procedures sportsperson to be dull, safe, and blinkered.

Inevitably, at all levels of sport, it is useful to have both perspectives. This obviously applies to team sports but is also vital in individual sports as well. Just doing the same thing time after time will become non-effective, no matter how many times it has worked in the past. Equally, doing nothing but new things, off the cuff, will produce disastrous results.

10.3 Internal Or External

This Meta Program explains the basis of an individual's motivation. Some sportspeople obtain all the motivation they require from within themselves. No matter what is happening they seem to able to go inside, dig deep and find that extra something that makes all the difference.

Others are more externally-referenced and require lots of feedback on how they are doing. Other people's opinions are their main motivation. Starved of this, they may well lose their edge and level of performance. For them, feedback is not just based upon results but on the opinion of others. This may include the coach, team-mates, press, and crowds.

Profile: Internally-referenced Sportspeople

How to recognise them:

- they seem to be very self-absorbed and unaware of how other team-mates are feeling
- they tend to analyse their own reactions and responses a great deal, often without seeking feedback
- if they get feedback from others that doesn't match their own view, they may question the validity of the other person's view
- they tend not to reveal much (unless you know the signs) in their gestures or non-verbal communication

In coaching or supporting them:

- create rapport by showing them that you understand them (but don't go overboard on building a relationship as they may well misconstrue this and withdraw)
- be very explicit when communicating with them
- do not take any of their reactions personally or get drawn into trying to change them
- be very specific and to-the-point when giving them feedback or asking them to do something

Profile: Externally-referenced Sportspeople

How to recognise them:

- they seek other people's opinions and views
- they have difficulty in starting or continuing something e.g. without some external input
- they tend to show their levels of agreement by gestures, nodding and non-verbal communication
- they take note of how other team-mates or colleagues are feeling
- they may become the team spokesperson (or at least be up-front in sharing their views)
- they tend to be happy if everyone is (and negative if everyone is down)

In coaching or supporting them:

- be enthusiastic about some aspect of their performance
- don't give them bad news all the time
- use words and phrases like *we, us, all, everybody, the team*
- listen to their opinions and answer all their questions
- pick up on any disagreements they are involved in
- pay attention to them outside the normal conventions of the relationship, e.g. over a break or outside training
- eat and drink with them
- show how other people have responded positively to circumstances
- show respect for them and the rest of the team

One of the greatest frustrations for an individual sportsperson is being unsure as to why they do something, or why some things seem more important than others do. The beauty of the Meta Programs is that they explain aspects of personality and motivation that many sportspeople are only vaguely aware of.

In particular, recognising your source of motivation is obviously vital. It allows you to recognise what works for you and then use it to your advantage. In team sports, the source of motivation can also explain how cliques and factions can appear, whilst some individuals go their own way.

For a manager or coach it is really useful to be able to put a structure and explanation on certain behaviours. It is important to point out that the manager or coach does not need to agree with the individual sportsperson's preference. The value lies in recognising it, respecting it, and acting appropriately.

10.4 Sameness Or Difference

This Meta Program relates to the individual's need or desire for change and how frequently change is required. Depending on the degree of this desire for change, people tend to focus on either similarities or differences.

Change is an important factor in sport, e.g.:

- a change in diet
- a change in training activities
- new tactics to be absorbed
- new team-mates to respond to
- new teams coming through
- changing personal circumstances

The capacity for change in sport is endless, and the individual's preferred response is a vital factor in how effectively it is handled.

Profile: Sportspeople With A Sameness-preference

These sportspeople hope that things will stay the same. They may defend the traditional way things have been, and their acceptance of change may be slow and grudging. They are unwilling to initiate change or to adopt new skills and techniques.

How to recognise them:

- they tend to look for the similarity in situations and techniques and want to build on those similarities
- they will look for consistency in methods and tactics
- they will be conservative and take time to accept new ways of doing things
- their language will include words like *same, like, common, similar*
- they tend to focus on what is working

In coaching or supporting them:

- communicate shared goals
- build on the similarities between the new and the old
- use their previous knowledge and expertise to move forward
- show them how the new is only built on the old, not debasing it or undervaluing it
- use words like *develop* rather than *change*

Profile: Sportspeople With A Difference-preference

These sportspeople love change. Nothing can change too quickly for them. What is not changing cannot be right. They love to vary training or tactics and to learn new skills. They constantly need new roles or responsibilities to keep them motivated.

How to recognise them:

- they constantly seek out new ways
- they compare everything, looking for the difference

- they use words like *new, different, changed, better, transformed*
- they tend to be more interested in what is happening next than what is happening now
- they like to be different, an individual
- they will look for what isn't working

In coaching or supporting them:

- emphasise the newness of training, tactics and methods, show them how new changes will make the situation better
- point out improvements
- use words and phrases like *new, unique, first time, different, first, unheard of*
- say things like, 'I don't know if you can do this', which will challenge them to show that they can

This Meta Program helps to explain why some people seem to be set in their ways, while others are up for anything new (sometimes irritatingly so!). There may be value in assisting sameness sportspeople with changes while at the same time slowing down difference people who may want change for change's sake.

10.5 Proactive Or Reactive

In management circles the accepted wisdom is that proactive people are better than reactive ones, as they make things happen. With Meta Programs this is not necessarily the case. The value of distinguishing between proactive and reactive people lies in understanding them and so helping them to achieve more.

Profile: Proactive Sportspeople

Proactive sportspeople will start things happening, often without waiting to check how others feel. They will start the job and get it done but sometimes this will upset others who feel they have been 'steamrollered' without consideration.

How to recognise them:

- they are very direct in their speech and actions
- they get right to the point
- they use active language
- they speak from a position of control over their own circumstances
- they may 'steamroller' other team-mates

In coaching or supporting them:

- give them clear instructions
- don't interfere if something is working
- keep them active and occupied
- let them start and finish something
- don't slow them down with over-analysis

Profile: Reactive Sportspeople

Reactive sportspeople wait before acting, preferring to consider and analyse before responding. Sometimes they will not actually take any action, feeling that merely thinking about something is enough. This can irritate and annoy others of a more proactive nature. Some reactive people believe that everything is a matter of luck, therefore there is no point in acting too soon.

How to recognise them:

- they tend to hang back from taking action
- they analyse thoroughly before giving a commitment to act
- they need reassurance that something will work before acting
- they tend to need more and more information
- they express their belief in luck and things just happening

In coaching or supporting them:

- give them time to think
- allow them to have lots of information

- don't press for decisions too quickly
- allow them to follow other people's lead
- allow them time to present their opinions in their own slightly longer way
- try not to hurry them up too much

This Meta Program can cause lots of confusion and occasionally some ill-feeling, but each aspect is valid in its own way. It would not be helpful if everyone was proactive, constantly leaping in, making things happen, racing ahead. Equally a team of reactive people would tend to wait too long before acting, seeking more information before acting or responding.

Like some of the other Meta Programs this is one where sometimes opposites attract. Within the little groups that can occur in a team often the proactive and reactive types will get together. It is as though each fulfils the other's need. In the team discussions it can be interesting to pair up a proactive player with a reactive player. However, this should be done for a positive reason and a careful eye should be kept on the dynamics of the process.

10.6 Big Picture Or Detail

Some sportspeople like large pieces (or chunks) of information that convey the whole picture. Others prefer step-by-step details and would be put off by getting the whole picture too soon.

Profile: Big-picture Sportspeople

These sportspeople will ask for, and give, the big picture, becoming quickly bored by too many details.
How to recognise them:

- they tend to seek out the big picture
- they talk in generalities rather than specifics

- they are comfortable with big ideas, concepts and abstract issues
- they will not give, or seek, lots of details
- they tend to move from idea to idea without necessarily linking them
- they become bored easily

In coaching or supporting them:

- give them the big picture or objective first
- keep your conversation (and training, etc.) varied by using a wide range of words and techniques
- avoid too much detail, too soon
- summarise big points
- use short, sharp, simple sentences
- watch for what makes them bored
- use words and phrases like *big picture, framework, concept, generally*

Profile: Detail Sportspeople

Sportspeople with this preference like everything to be detailed, logical and step-by-step. They do not like being forced into making decisions or coming to conclusions without all the information being available. They do not like generalities and prefer lots of examples. Sometimes they find it hard to prioritise their needs.

How to recognise them:

- they ask for lots of details
- they like things to be prepared in a step-by-step way
- if they lose their way in an explanation or a question they tend to start all over again
- they tend to use lots of adverbs and adjectives
- they become frustrated by lots of generalisations

In coaching or supporting them:

- give them information and instructions in a detailed, step-by-step way

- be prepared to take questions about details
- use precise language
- use words like *specifically, exactly, first, second, third*
- get them to come up with a plan for themselves in order to implement ideas or actions

Unlike in the other Meta Programs, where people may change their patterns in different contexts, people who like the big picture tend to do so in all contexts, and, similarly, people who prefer details tend to do so across contexts.

10.7 Stress Response: Feelings/Choices/Thinking

This can be a particularly useful Meta Program for the sportsperson. Some people may feel that it is only at the professional level that players become stressed, but this is not necessarily the case. This Meta Program has three categories, rather than two polarities.

Stress impacts on sportspeople in different ways. Something that will totally stress one person will not affect another at all. This is complicated by the fact that some people who appear to be stress-free are actually bottling it up as their particular way of controlling stress. The case of Paul Gascoigne in the autumn of 1998 is an example of this. Superficially, in spite of all his problems, he always appeared to be an easy-going 'jack the lad' character. However, beneath the surface there were lots of unresolved issues fermenting away, which finally resulted in his visiting a clinic.

Profile: Feelings-response Sportspeople

Sportspeople with this profile can be highly intuitive and creative but also volatile and erratic in their behaviour. They do not like negative feedback and can react quite forcibly to it, so they can cause friction with sportspeople who respond to stress in a thinking way.

How to recognise them:

- they tend to use animated gestures and body-language, making particular use of their arms, body, facial expressions and voice
- they may remain emotional for some time, even after events seem to have moved on
- they can 'ignite' very quickly

In coaching or supporting them:

- pay attention to their emotions instead of responding to their emotions with cold logic and facts
- allow them to get things off their chest
- empathise with their concerns
- be assertive both verbally and non-verbally, holding eye contact, and talking about *we* not *I*
- show them the positive intention in your response

Profile: Choices-response Sportspeople

These sportspeople may start out by responding to a situation in an emotional way, then quickly returning to their normal unemotional response. Their emotional response is less overt or intense than the sportsperson who responds with feelings.

How to recognise them:

- they display an initial emotional response quickly followed by a more measured, normal one
- they may show a degree of empathy
- they will often be the spokesperson for a group in a stressful situation
- they tend to exhibit signs of being in control

In coaching or supporting them:

- allow their initial emotional response to die down before responding
- listen to both their emotional and non-emotional responses
- don't react differently to the emotional and non-emotional parts

- create empathy with them
- display and share your own preferred style with them

Profile: Thinking-response Sportspeople

These people display a non-emotional response to a situation that normally other sportspeople would find stressful. They remain calm and impassive, irrespective of anyone else's response.

How to recognise them:

- they show no visible negative responses to stress in words, voice tone or body-language
- they tend not to panic
- they stick to the facts
- they seem to be unaware or uncaring of the people around them who are responding differently

In coaching or supporting them:

- stick to the facts
- control your own responses, i.e. do not batter them with your own emotional responses and expect them to react
- ask them questions to draw out their thinking
- get them to offer solutions, then analyse their responses

The power of this Meta Program is that it can help explain why a particular sportsperson reacts in a certain way and how best they can either help themselves or be helped by someone else.

10.8 Style: Independence/Proximity/Co-operation

This Meta Program can be very revealing, particularly in team sports. An easy assumption is that sportspeople who play team sports do so partially because they like to play with others and that this therefore allows them to give of their best. This is not necessarily true, as some people prefer to do it their way even when playing within a team.

Profile: Sportspeople Who Prefer Independence

These sportspeople prefer to work on their own. This often means that in training they will prefer to do things alone and for themselves. They are quite happy to take responsibility for their own actions. They will work with others, but they feel uncomfortable if this adversely affects their own performance.

How to recognise them:

- they tend to create their own routines and tasks
- they do not contribute a great deal in open discussions about other people
- their language tends to be based on themselves, i.e. *me, my, I, myself, alone*
- they will stand up for themselves even in a team situation with collective responsibilities

In coaching or supporting them:

- create rapport by recognising their independence
- use individual rather than collective words
- give them individual responsibilities within the team's objectives
- give them individual feedback based on their performance

Profile: Sportspeople Who Prefer Proximity

As with sportspeople who prefer independence, those who prefer proximity like to have responsibilities clearly established. However, these people want others to be either involved or at least close by, even if their proximity is not always acknowledged.

How to recognise them:

- they show a need for other people
- they want a clear role, tasks and accountabilities when working with others
- their effectiveness may be affected by having to share responsibility with others

In coaching or supporting them:

- give them clear roles, tasks and accountabilities
- involve them in working with others
- keep other people around them
- don't allow other people to divert them from what they are trying to achieve

Profile: Sportspeople Who Prefer Co-operation

As the name suggests, this preference is rooted in the desire to work with other sportspeople or colleagues and to share duties and responsibilities. These sportspeople are firmly committed to teamwork. If for some reason they have to do something on their own they may have some trouble achieving completion.

How to recognise them:

- they are fully involved with and committed to others
- they are bothered by the 'independents'
- they will do anything for others or for the team
- they tend to express or show uncertainty when asked to do something on their own
- they tend to use words like *us, we, all, together*

In coaching or supporting them:

- keep them training and working with others
- allow them some freedom with others
- develop shared roles, responsibilities and accountabilities
- keep a careful eye on them when they are working alone
- show how what they are doing will benefit the team

Having the personal insight into recognising style preference can be very helpful for the sportsperson. It can help explain why people train, prepare and even play the way they do. It can also explain some of the cliques and factions that can occur in sports.

10.9 Organisation: Things Or People

This Meta Program is about whether the sportsperson pays more attention to things or to people. In this context, things mean ideas, systems, plans, procedures, or processes. For example, in reviewing a performance, sportspeople who are thing-orientated will be more interested in examining if the plan worked or if the tasks were achieved, without being too interested in how people felt. Sportspeople who are person-orientated, on the other hand, will be very aware of the feelings of others, and will place a lot of importance on them.

Profile: Thing-orientated Sportspeople

Even in a team situation, these sportspeople tend to place all their attention and emphasis on the structure, plan, procedures and goals. If they mention people at all it is in an indirect or detached way.

How to recognise them:

- they tend to focus on procedures, plans, goals, systems
- they hardly mention people at all
- they see people as part of the plan, like components, unit or objects
- they tend to be unemotional (although they can be emotional in their own particular way)

In coaching or supporting them:

- stick to procedures and plans etc.
- use lots of facts
- get them to share facts and ideas with you
- be clear about how they would prefer things to be done
- don't impede their progress
- get to them to share their goals and methods with others

Profile: People-orientated Sportspeople

These sportspeople are at ease with others and have a good awareness of how others view things.

How to recognise them:

- they will talk about and reflect team-mates' and others' views and opinions
- they use words and phrases like *we, us, all, consider others' opinions, what would help us*
- they tend to make you feel at ease with them
- they will often be at the centre of things
- they will be up-front about their own feelings and opinions

In coaching or supporting them:

- reflect their type of language back to them
- focus on how people will make the plan work and goals be achieved
- show how their role will help others
- show them that you have understood how they feel about the plan or system
- be open about your own feelings and emotions
- use names of people frequently in your discussions

Many people who manage or coach teams see themselves as equally balanced between things and people. For the individual sportsperson it can be helpful to recognise your own preference so that you can make best use of it.

10.10 Convincer Channel

There are two facets to how a sportsperson becomes convinced about something. One is the convincer channel, which is about whether we need to see, hear or read information, or perform an action, in order to be convinced. The other facet is the convincer pattern, which is explained further on in this chapter.

Profile: Sportspeople with a Seeing Preference

Nothing convinces these people unless they actually see it happen. This can mean that it actually happens in reality, or they see it happening in their mind's eye. For them to be convinced of the value of a tactic, game plan or idea, they will prefer to see it presented *visually*.

Profile: Sportspeople with a Hearing Preference

These sportspeople need to hear about something if they are to be convinced. In receiving instructions or information they will prefer words presented orally. They will be influenced by how something is *said*.

Profile: Sportspeople with a Reading Preference

Words and pictures mean little to these sportspeople, who like to see things in a written form. They prefer to *read* information in order to become convinced and like giving attention to the written word.

Profile: Sportspeople with a Doing Preference

None of the other three convincer-channels will work for this sportsperson as well as actually *doing* something. If it is a person they need to be convinced about, they will want to work with that person. If it is a plan or a tactic, they will want to try it out, demonstrate it for themselves. Even seeing someone else demonstrating something won't convince them, as they need to do it themselves.

10.11 Convincer Pattern

This Meta Program explains the process the sportsperson goes through in order to become convinced about the validity of something. This is a highly individual pattern and yet most sportspeople assume everyone else does it the same way that they do. This preference is particularly important because of its impact on learning and acquiring new skills and methods.

Profile: Sportspeople with an Automatic Preference

These sportspeople will make very quick decisions based on a small amount of information.

How to recognise them:

- they decide on something very quickly
- they do not ask for a lot of evidence
- they assume that information must be right
- they do not change their mind very easily

In coaching or supporting them:

- allow them to make decisions at their own speed
- give them high-quality information quickly
- don't be put off by the speed of their decisions
- show empathy by giving them the benefit of the doubt
- don't over-burden them with lots of information

Profile: Sportspeople with a Consistent Preference

These sportspeople are the opposite of those who operate on an automatic preference. No matter how many times something occurs or how many examples they have, they are never really convinced.

How to recognise them:

- they are painstaking in their evaluation of something, e.g. a game plan, or a new tactic
- they will go back to the beginning and query something even when everybody else has accepted it
- they don't want to be hurried
- every time something happens they will judge it as if it is the first time

In coaching or supporting them:

- allow them as much time as is possible
- stay calm, patient and neutral with them

- always start from the beginning when explaining any theory
- go at their speed
- explain everything without skipping any details

Profile: Sports Person with a Number-of-examples Preference

These sportspeople like to have a number of examples before becoming convinced.

How to recognise them:

- they will keep asking for explanations or examples
- they will be uncomfortable if insufficient examples are offered
- they may require a specific number of examples

In coaching or supporting them:

- recognise the specific number of examples they require
- be prepared to provide the number they require
- be prepared for the questions they may ask
- don't rush them

Profile: Sportspeople with a Period-of-time Preference

Similar to the number-of-examples preference, these sportspeople like a particular period of time to absorb and accept things.

How to recognise them:

- they tend to need, or ask for, a certain amount of time
- they will show frustration if things are being rushed
- they tend to show evidence that they are absorbing things by thinking and asking questions

In coaching or supporting them:

- recognise the particular length of time they require
- be prepared to provide a vast amount of time
- be prepared for the questions they may ask
- don't rush them

This convincer pattern can be very revealing of your approach. Most of us are unaware of what our preference is, but recognising our patterns can help us to ensure that we become properly convinced before acting. It is also helpful for a manager or coach to recognise these preferences and respond accordingly.

This is one of the longest chapters in this book, and for good reasons. Meta Programs reveal the drivers for sportspeople's behaviour i.e. they explain *why* they do *what* they do. As always, paying attention and listening will provide a huge amount of useful information that can be used to create a successful approach.

You can use information about the Meta Programs that you follow to arrange circumstances to suit your preferences or develop more flexible approaches to widen your skill base. This level of self-awareness and understanding can help you to make a significant improvement in your performance.

For anyone dealing with sportspeople, e.g. a manager or coach, it is obviously helpful to understand every aspect of what 'makes someone tick'. Equally, an awareness of their own preferences can help them become more effective in their roles.

Chapter 11

Develop Strategies For Success

All of us use some form of strategy to achieve success. Our strategy may be based on some prior knowledge of the opponent, or on a desire to achieve certain levels of performance. Even just playing to have fun can be defined as a form of strategy. Some of our strategies are overt and explicit, but there may be many that we are unaware of.

Strategies are an important factor in everything that human beings do. As mentioned earlier in this book, the early developments in NLP were based on the strategies that various successful people employed, often without their being consciously aware of them.

There is enormous scope for further research using NLP techniques to help establish what the great 'natural' sportspeople do that makes them so successful, and how they do it.

Within NLP there are techniques for establishing the 'how's of any human process. This is known as modelling, and a large part of any NLP training consists of practising modelling strategies.

One of the fascinating findings of modelling strategies is that we also have strategies for the things we believe we cannot do. Modelling means that we can reproduce someone else's sports skill as part of our own performance. This does not mean that every cricketer can be an Ian Botham or every footballer a Michael Owen, but it does mean that parts of what they do can be added to anyone's game.

Essentially all human behaviour is based on some form of strategy, from getting up in the morning, to driving a car, or writing a letter.

The three components of a strategy are:

- the beliefs that support the behaviour
- the physiology of the behaviour
- the strategies that support the behaviour

The NLP process of finding out someone's strategy can be described as follows:

1. Identify the specific behaviour, e.g. taking a penalty, serving an ace, holing a putt.
2. Get the sportsperson to actually do the behaviour. If this is not possible, get them to go back in time to when they were successfully carrying out the behaviour and get them totally into the state of doing it, in an associated way.
3. Identify the very first thing they are aware of as they are reliving the experience.
4. Find out specifically what they see, hear, feel etc.
5. Identify the second thing they are aware of as they are reliving the behaviour.
6. Find out specifically what they see, hear, feel, etc.
7. Repeat for each specific part of the behaviour until you have worked out their total strategy.

There are two kinds of modelling: body modelling and mind modelling.

Body Modelling

Most people use some form of body modelling to learn a new skill. Children learning to walk copy what they see around them, mainly from their parents. They have an unconscious awareness of what is required to walk, from observing, before it is actually explained to them. Many skills are taught or learnt to some extent by modelling. People who have never thrown a javelin or hurdled or played golf have a good idea of what is involved physically. In cricket when Jeff Thompson, the Australian fast bowler, was playing, every child on a street corner bowled like him. Andrew Caddick, the Somerset and England bowler, has modelled himself on the great New Zealand bowler Richard Hadlee.

In NLP there is a structured process for body modelling:

- choose a good role model
- make sure that when you are modelling them they are doing it right (even the greats have an off-day)
- get a picture locked in your head of them performing perfectly (the use of video is obviously helpful here), make sure that you can reproduce their perfect performance in your mind's eye

- see yourself carrying out the skill / performance in *exactly* the same way as the role model
- step *inside* the picture (become associated) and be more aware of how it looks , sounds, feels, smells and tastes to perform perfectly
- practise this five or six times a day

This process covers the physiological aspects of a player's performance, but ignores their beliefs and strategies.

This may explain why Andrew Caddick, although a high quality county player, was not selected for the 1998/9 England tour of Australia. The reason given was a lack of mental toughness, (something that Richard Hadlee was never accused of!). In other words, Andrew Caddick can model Richard Hadlee's action and delivery but, without sharing Hadlee's beliefs and strategies, he will never achieve the same heights.

Mind Modelling

The key steps are:

- break the sports performance down into its key elements
- break it down into even smaller chunks if required
- observe the process (possibly using a video), and interview the sportsperson to establish their:
  - beliefs
  - values
  - attitudes
  - thought patterns

For the purpose of the book it is not necessary to be NLP-trained or to know or understand the modelling process. Any sportsperson or coach who wants to be able to do this can either attend a training course or read some of the appropriate NLP literature. In this book we will be developing processes based on the NLP techniques but without using all of the jargon that normally goes with them.

> *And Warne or no Warne, as far as I am concerned,*
> *the Ashes will be won or lost in the mind.*
> *Daily Mail* 1998 commentary on the 1998/9
> England Cricket Tour of Australia.

A strategy is like a game-plan or blueprint for action and should include all aspects of what is likely to occur. This means planning for the things that may go right or wrong, and being sufficiently mentally and physically prepared to be able to deal with anything that happens.

A plan can also be used to ensure that training achieves maximum benefit. It is astonishing how many sportspeople, at all levels, will have some form of game-plan for the event itself but none for the training, *which is the means to achieving the end*. More and more people involved in sport are now recognising that the mental aspects of the training process are as important as the physical. Some sportspeople hate training, seeing it as something that has to be done, waiting only for the actual event itself. Others, however, seem to be able to produce their best in training and struggle to establish consistent levels of performance outside the training area.

> *In my experience confidence has come from knowing the hard work has been put in. Like money into a bank account, without the deposit, there is no withdrawal.*
>
> Sharron Davies

It is vital to have a strategy for success in training. This allows people who do not enjoy training to measure their progress, to enjoy it and to develop the link between training and the actual event. It also helps sportspeople who struggle to take their training performance into the competition to focus on what they need to do to bridge the gap.

The six key stages for which you need a strategy are:

- prior to training
- training
- the build-up between training and the event
- the event itself
- reviewing the event
- planning for next time

For each of the stages a simple checklist can be developed. If you do not like the idea of having a structured list to follow, try following the process for a period until you no longer need the list except as a reminder.

Activity

Think about the answers to these questions:

- What skill/tactics do I want to practise at training?
- What will be the evidence/measures of my success?
- What specific actions do I need to take to practise the skills or tactics?
- What beliefs do I have regarding my ability to achieve the improved level?
- What NLP techniques can I use prior to training to ensure success (e.g. mental rehearsal, visualisation, affirmation, relaxation etc.)?

Activity

Think about your answers to these questions:

- How will I carry forward the work undertaken into the training itself?
- Who else do I need to involve, e.g. coach, team-mates?
- What are the mental aspects of my game I want to work on in training? For example, do I want to work on my beliefs, anchors, self-confidence, hanging on when the going gets tough, dealing with interference factors, concentration, developing positive self-talk?
- What will be the measures of my success in the five senses, i.e. what will I see, hear, feel, smell or taste when I have succeeded?
- What will be the physical measures of my success?
- How will I reward myself for my success?
- What is my action plan to take forward between training and the actual event?

Activity

Think about your answers to these questions:

- What am I choosing to work on at this stage?
- How can I plan my time in order to ensure that I use it purposefully?
- What relaxation techniques will I use?
- What can I do to keep myself occupied and focused?
- What do I need to know about my opponent(s), the venue, travel arrangements, or anything else that could distract me?
- What individual/team tactics do I need to pay attention to?

Activity

Think about your answers to these questions:

- What specific part of my game am I using well?
- What part of my game do I need to pay more attention to?
- What do I need to take into account regarding my opponent, the environment, my team-mates?
- What can I do to achieve success today?
- Am I enjoying the game?
- What NLP techniques am I using (e.g. beliefs, anchoring, self-confidence, hanging on when the going gets tough, dealing with interference factors, improved concentration, developing positive self-talk)?
- What other NLP techniques would be helpful?
- How aware am I of my five senses?
- How am I responding to this information?

Activity

Think about your answers to these questions:

- What worked well for me?
- What do I need to work on further?
- Who else do I need to involve?
- What specific parts of the performance do I need to re-visualise, store away, develop anchors for?
- What specific part of the performance do I need to analyse and build into my beliefs about my ability, my self-talk, the affirmations I can use?
- What setbacks did I overcome and how can I use them to work for me the next time?
- What did I learn about myself that I didn't know already?
- What do I need to remember about my opponent, the environment, etc. for the next time?
- What can I do to improve my levels of success next time?
- How will I measure the improved levels of success?

Activity

Think about your answers to these questions:

- What do I specifically want to work on prior to my next training, at the training or at any other stage of the process?
- How will I measure my success?
- Who else do I need to involve?
- What are my action steps between now and the next training?
- What do I want to work on (if anything) that I haven't previously tried?
- What else can I do to ensure I have fun and succeed?

Chapter 12

Recognise The Signals Of Success

It might sound odd to suggest that the amateur or professional sportsperson should acknowledge their improvement in performance. However, it is intriguing how many either seem not to spot the difference, or notice it but discount it and place emphasis only on other areas that could be improved.

In working with managers in organisations it is amazing how difficult it is to get more than lip-service regarding positive reinforcement – to actually get them doing it. This is possibly because so many people feel uncomfortable about receiving praise, tending either to deny their expertise modestly or to find negative reasons about why praise was given.

Evidence suggests that balanced feedback containing positive reinforcement works effectively. Many people use the feedback sandwich:

- giving specific feedback on an issue or skill
- giving specific feedback on an area to work on or develop
- agreeing a positive direction

This is a simple, unsophisticated model that also enhances the relationship between colleagues and between sportsperson and coach.

Some people find it difficult to differentiate between feedback and criticism. The key differences are:

- Criticism focuses on the person, whereas feedback focuses on the behaviour or the situation.
- Criticism is general, whereas feedback is specific.
- Criticism evaluates, blames and finds fault, while feedback describes and seeks remedies.
- Criticism dwells on what happened in the past, while feedback emphasises what will be done in the future.

It is also worth pointing out that both criticism and feedback are not just received from an external source. Both may be delivered internally through internal dialogue or self-talk and, although not heard by anyone else, it frequently causes more long-term damage than feedback received from others.

Of course recognising signals of success is not just about feedback. It needs to be based on something substantial. The obvious ways of recognising signals is through measured performance, but this will only indicate the improvement, not necessarily how it was achieved. Knowing how it was achieved will make it possible to repeat it.

As already stated, within NLP a great deal of attention is paid to how we receive and respond to information provided by the five senses: visual, auditory, kinaesthetic, olfactory, and gustatory. Sportspeople will know through their senses what it looks, sounds and feels like to get some things right. This analysis will be a combination of obvious factors, e.g. in cricket seeing the ball onto the bat, hearing the sound as the ball hits the centre of the bat, recognising the feel in the arms and body when everything is working properly. But it goes a lot deeper than that. It is possible to recognise and develop the internal signals of successful performance.

Sportspeople will often talk about feeling just right (or not) on the day. These internal factors can be isolated, worked on and honed. In the same way that proper physical repetition would enable the body to respond appropriately, mental repetition can achieve the same objective.

> *It was all mental. I kept focused and fought for every point. I never gave up and took it point by point and tried to stay positive. It took a while but eventually I started to play a little bit smarter.*
>
> Mary Pierce after defeating Martina Hingis in a tennis tournament.

When sportspeople talk about feeling right, that's normally exactly what they mean. Through a combination of the senses the mind becomes prepared and the performance of the body follows on.

Therefore in the same way that they work on recognising the signals of physical success, the sportsperson needs to pay as much attention to recognising the signals of success through the senses. The following activities will help you to develop the skills.

Activity

- After a successful performance analyse through the five senses what you saw, heard, felt, smelt or tasted *at the time of peak performance.*
- Note whatever internal dialogue/self-talk was taking place and the impact it had.
- Practise re-creating the signals of success in your mental warm-ups and mental rehearsal.

Activity

- Do the above for a non-sporting context as well. Find the signals.
- Use the NLP process of anchoring (explained in chapter 7) to cross the use of these signals into a sporting situation.

Chapter 13

Harness Greater Self-awareness

You have to be totally honest with yourself.
Kevin Keegan

To achieve a balance in all aspects of our lives, a good degree of self-awareness, which includes realism regarding our impact on others, is a distinct advantage. In sport the ability to be honest with ourselves about progress, achievement, attitudes to training, etc. really does make some crucial differences. Some sportspeople put all their energy into focusing on the opponent, sometimes to the exclusion of everything else. This, of course, is not always necessarily wrong. In some sports, e.g. boxing or tennis, understanding the opponent's game, their strengths and weaknesses, how they handle key moments of pressure, their likely response to some of the things we might do, are absolutely vital and require as much research and preparation as any other part of our game.

However, the difference that makes the difference is very often understanding ourselves, what we are trying to do and the options we have available to us.

One of the best-known stories that illustrate this is the Mohammed Ali fight with George Foreman in Zaire in 1974. In the build-up to the fight none of the sports commentators gave Ali a chance. In fact many were worried about his physical safety, convinced that he would suffer permanent damage. Ali's words about what he would do to Foreman were dismissed as empty rhetoric, the babbling of someone in love with himself who was unaware of his own fallibility and limitations, and was under-estimating his opponent.

At that time Foreman was unbeaten, he had knocked out virtually all of his opponents. He had obliterated Joe Frazier, who had beaten Ali, in such a decisive manner that it had enhanced his aura of invincibility. Equally importantly, he regarded himself as unbeatable.

This was not self-delusion or hype. He had the amateur and professional record to prove his point. He knew that he was the most effective puncher in world boxing and had total belief in his ability to get to his opponents both physically and mentally. All who saw the pre-fight interviews and press conferences loved the humour of Ali but were impressed by the absolute conviction that Foreman possessed.

Everyone said that the only chance Ali had, which wasn't much of a chance at all, was to dance, back off and keep out of trouble. But no one believed that he could do it for 15 rounds.

The first round of the fight confirmed everyone's opinion. Foreman came forward throwing massive punches; Ali danced, weaved and kept moving. In the film *When We Were Kings*, which chronicles the build-up to the fight Norman Mailer, the American writer, states that at the end of the first round Ali knew what he up against. He knew nothing he had done before, all the skills developed and acquired over the years, would help to beat his opponent. Something different was required and Ali had to believe he could do it. To carry out the strategy of allowing the best puncher in the world to deliberately punch himself out on you would be considered madness by anybody. To do it with the full glare of the world looking on, with your opponent receiving feedback from your actions that there could only be one result, bordered on madness or even suicide in many people's eyes.

The result has become part of sporting history. By seeming to play to his opponent's strengths Ali achieved one of the biggest surprises in boxing history. Once Foreman's approach did not achieve the expected results he didn't know what else to do. His physical strategy was to carry on swinging heavy punches, expending energy, while at the same time being taunted by Ali, who kept talking to him in their clinches, asking, 'Is that the best you've got, George'? Mentally Foreman did not know how to respond. He was locked into one pattern, which he kept repeating, until in the end he was defeated.

There has been much speculation over the years as to whether Ali's tactics were established before the fight. Mailer is convinced they were the result of the first round and the realisation that something different and special was required. Ali has always said that he knew that no matter what Foreman did he would be able to handle it and respond appropriately.

The one thing that is undeniable is that Ali's awareness of self, his absolute conviction that he could read a situation and know that he could respond, was the one factor that made all the difference. Apart from the obvious physical aspects, the fight had been won in the mind, by someone whose sense of self-awareness was developed to an extremely high degree, which allowed him to choose an appropriate response which he believed he could carry through.

In this section focus will be given to two specific aspects of self-awareness:

- self-expectation
- self-image

Most sportspeople are aware of the concept of a self-fulfilling prophecy. This means if we think we cannot do something, that is normally exactly what happens. Within sport psychology there is a lot of evidence that, because of the mind-body connection, the body will deliver what the mind has determined. Therefore, being clear about what *can* be achieved and then dealing with how to achieve it is a vital skill.

Activity

Think about your answers to these questions:

- On balance, do I look for the positive in a situation or focus on the negative?
- Would people who know me well describe me as an optimist or pessimist?
- Is what I show on the outside consistent with what I am feeling and believing on the inside?
- Do I treat temporary difficulties as exactly that, or do I allow them to build and develop into something bigger (and maybe more permanent)?
- Do I indulge in self-pity when something goes wrong?
- At the end of an event do I tend to focus on what went well or what didn't?
- Do I use positive self-talk (internal dialogue) before, during and after performance?
- Do I see the positive in other people or situations, or do the negatives come more naturally to me?
- Are my friends, colleagues and team-mates naturally positive or negative? What impact does this have on me?

A specific NLP technique for dealing with self-expectation is establishing personal outcomes (covered earlier).

Train to the highest level of fitness you can achieve. Then believe in yourself. Go to the start of your race knowing that you are as ready both mentally and physically as you will ever be.

Sally Gunnell

Self-image is normally very deeply rooted and created by childhood experiences. All of the evidence indicates that there are strong links between behaviour, performance and self-image.The developments within NLP have made it even clearer how big a part self-image plays. A number of NLP techniques address this issue, either directly or indirectly.

Activity

Think about your answers to these questions:

- Do I have a vision or dream for my sports performance in the future?
- Do I allow myself to daydream about how I would achieve my vision?
- Have I taken an audit of all my skills and talents, including the ones that, at this stage, appear not to have any immediate relevance or use?
- Do I convey a positive self-image to others? Is it consistent with what I believe inside about myself?
- What are the things that I believe I am not good at? What is the evidence for this? Why do I choose to believe this?
- Are the images I have of myself consistent with what I am going to achieve?

Activity

Establish a pattern whereby you set aside about 10 minutes a day to visualise yourself achieving sporting success. Ensure that you are associated, i.e. inside the event. Be clear about what you see, hear, feel, taste and smell. It may help to have suitable soft music in the background. Baroque or chamber music works effectively for some sportspeople.

Activity

Listen to tapes or read books about high achievers. Notice how they use their self-image to make things work for them. There are lots of books and tapes available by or about sportspeople, but don't restrict yourself to these. Investigate people from any walk of life who fascinate you.

Activity

Use positive affirmations in the morning and last thing at night.

Activity

Use autogenic training (explained in chapter 25, ***Use Relaxation Techniques***).

Activity

Take the lead in team discussions. Break up normal pattern.

Activity

Give other team-mates, friends or colleagues feedback on how you perceive them. Encourage them to give you feedback on how they perceive you. Use this feedback to further enhance your self-image.

Activity

Write down (or speak into a tape) your outcomes, dreams and aspirations. Play or re-read these on a regular basis and update them as appropriate. Integrate them into your life.

Activity

Tell other people what you are doing to build your self-image. It is not necessary to work alone on this issue.

Activity

Get used to analysing your strengths and successes. Plan specifically how to develop them further.

Activity

Practise paying attention to your language. Do you tend more toward visual, auditory or kinaesthetic language? Does this differ depending on whether you are discussing successes or failures? Is the language you use with others consistent with your internal dialogue?

Activity

Get used to talking yourself up, realistically, through your internal dialogue.

Chapter 14

Process Relevant Information

Information can be received in many different ways. There is information from the five senses, i.e. what we see, hear, feel, smell and taste.

In addition there is all sorts of other information to be processed such as the size and shape of the venue, the proximity of any spectators, or the noise the spectators produce. Dealing with information about our own nervous state is also important both before and during the actual game.

Our internal dialogue will also be relaying all sorts of messages, and the coach or team-mates will also be putting out messages which need to be analysed, sorted and responded to.

The danger in all this is, of course, information-overload. Most of us will have experienced our mind racing with everything it is trying to absorb and act on. This normally means that too little attention is directed towards key elements and the overall performance suffers. This is where use of the appropriate NLP techniques can be so useful.

Another important aspect of information-processing is the ability to place useful information in the memory-bank and the ability to be able to retrieve it at the time it is required. For example in tennis, how the opponent serves during a key point, in rugby the preferred ploy at set pieces, for a goalkeeper in football which side a penalty-taker prefers to shoot. These factors require appropriate use of memory skills.

In essence there are three levels of memory storage, which can be explained by use of NLP. The first is the sensory register where huge amounts of information are held for a very short time, normally about half a second, before being transferred to another level of memory or lost altogether. (A car journey where the driver needs to be taking in a great deal of information all of the time, but not necessarily using any of it, is an example of this).

The second level is short-term memory. This operates, for example, when we look up a telephone number and repeat it and rehearse it so that we can dial it. Short-term memory also deals with retrieving required information from long-term memory so that it can be acted upon immediately.

The capacity of our short-term memory is relatively small but it can be increased by the NLP technique of chunking up or generalising. Chunking up allows a lot of information to be stored under one general heading. For example, in rugby union when the hooker uses the previously agreed code of numbers to indicate a pattern of play, this code will trigger the pattern of play involving a number of other players. The information for this pattern will be carried and coded under the agreed set of numbers. When the code is announced it brings into short-term memory all the information required to carry out the necessary action.

Our long-term memory carries information virtually permanently. In fact, it sometimes actually becomes impossible to forget something, such as a memory of a specific occasion or experience in childhood. Most of us remember, from our school days the mnemonic 'Richard Of York Gave Battle In Vain' for the sequence and colours of the rainbow: red, orange, yellow, green, blue, indigo and violet. When sportspeople talk about having a bad memory, what they normally mean is that they have failed to place particular pieces of information into their long-term memory. It can be useful to practise doing this as a particular skill.

What sports psychologists call attentional focus is crucial. This means the ability to narrow or widen our attention to deal with whatever is necessary. In most sports where there are many tasks to be undertaken, the ability to focus on the key areas totally and at exactly the right time can make the difference between success and failure.

An example of this is the footballer about to make a pass. He needs to have a wide view of the field of play, where his teammates and opponents are, and who he actually wants to pass to. All of this requires a great deal of processing of information, all of which will be wasted if insufficient attention is paid specifically to passing the ball to maximum effect.

> *You have to be able to be aware of everything that is happening but also know what needs to be done.*
>
> Kevin Keegan

The activities below cover the three components of processing relevant information: use of the five senses, memory and attentional focus.

Activity

This activity increases our awareness of our five senses.

Find somewhere to sit comfortably. Breathe deeply, slowly and regularly and close your eyes. Check that your body is relaxed all over. Think back to a time when you knew you were performing well. Take yourself back to that time, notice what you are aware of. Be aware of how your feet feel on the ground. What can you hear from any spectators? What can you hear from the internal dialogue in your head? Notice if you are associated or dissociated. Are there any smells or tastes that you are aware of? What can you see? What in particular gets your attention? How do you feel inside?

In doing all of this don't search too hard, just become increasingly aware of what appears and enjoy finding out how you respond to it.

Activity

Think back to a time when you were performing well, and choose one aspect, e.g. hitting a ball cleanly with a tennis racket or catching a ball properly. Choose one of your senses and focus on it to the exclusion of everything else. Now intensify the sound, sight, feeling, smell or taste. Turn the sensation up or down, as if it can be done by turning up a dial. Notice that your senses are not static, you can play with the intensity and power of them. This means that the impact can be increased and developed (or minimised with an experience that didn't go as well as it might have done).

Activity

Practise improving your memory by choosing a number of random words connected with your sport e.g. club, footwear, ground, team-mates, ball. Link them with the most unusual visual images you can find. Find the most unusual and bizarre images you can as the brain finds these easier to retain. Now use the linked images to help you to remember the entire list of words.

Activity

Choose 15 to 20 random words connected with the successful application of your sport. Develop a story that connects all the words altogether. The story does not have to be written down or make sense in the normal way, in fact it is better if it doesn't.

This is because even though the story is nonsensical it will 'stick' in your memory and be difficult to dislodge. The brain likes to be stretched and will hold on to unusual things. Notice how long your story sticks in your mind.

Activity

Use memory pegs. Put simply, this means taking something that needs to be remembered and attaching to it a key picture or word. The association means that when the key picture or word is used, the memory comes attached to it.

Activity

Use mnemonics. Make up your own mnemonics to remember a sequence of actions or instruction.

Activity

Use anchors. Creating a positive anchor for sporting experiences helps improve both memory and sporting performance immeasurably.

Activity

Practise concentrating on the present moment, ignoring the past or future. By paying greater attention to people and events around you, you will develop the skill of tuning out interference factors.

Activity

Ensure that your attentional focus is regained after something has intervened, e.g. after a break, when distracted, when a mistake has been made or when play is not going exactly according to plan.

Activity

Revisit the plan you developed before the event. Get back into it, here in the present.

Activity

Notice where, either in your sport or outside, you can use attentional focus, e.g. when reading a book or when watching your favourite TV programme. Analyse how you do it, then transfer the skills into the key moments in your sport.

Activity

Use the thought-centring process covered by Richard A. Cox in his book *Sports Psychology, Concepts And Applications*:

- Replace any negative thought that comes into your mind with a positive one.
- Centre your attention internally while making minor adjustments to your internal state.
- Narrowly focus your attention externally on a task-relevant cue that is associated with superior performance.
- Execute the sports skill as soon as you have achieved a feeling of attentional control.

Chapter 15

Pay Attention To What Works

Many sportspeople, including professionals, allow themselves to focus only on the negative, e.g. what might go wrong, the skill of the opponent, the lack of skill on their own part. All of this is understandable. However, carried to excess, it can destroy the enjoyment of a sport.

This of course is not to say that working on weaknesses is wrong or unhelpful. Handled appropriately it is a vital part of improving sports performance. But it should not be allowed to become the only approach used. A number of great sportspeople – ranging from Ian Botham, the Liverpool football team of the Seventies through to the rowers Steve Redgrave and Matthew Pinsent – have had the inner belief that they can deal with anything that occurs and achieve either victory or a great performance from any circumstances. This level of conviction is not based on a fear of what might go wrong, but on a reasoned analysis of what works.

One of the basic ideas of NLP is to look for what works and then build on it. This can be done by focusing on submodalities. Submodalities are clear descriptions or distinctions within each sense (or representational system). For example, is the picture you see (with your visual sense) in colour or black and white? Is it clear or blurred? Is the sound you hear (with your auditory sense) loud or soft? If you hear a voice in your head, whose voice is it? Is the voice nearby or far away? Answers to all these questions describe the submodalities of an experience.

A memory of a really positive sporting experience may be bright, close, loud, and with feelings of excitement and breathlessness. Compare this with a really poor sports performance, where the memory may be further away, smaller, more blurred, quieter with very different feelings.

You never forget the big moments. They're burned into your mind.

Kevin Keegan

It may happen that it is the poor performance that is bright and clear, and the good performance that is blurred and far away. Should this be the case it is very revealing of how you are paying attention only to what didn't work. It is very effective to try to swap round the submodalities of the two memories, to make your memory of the good performance bright and clear and the poor performance blurred and far away.

The responsibility for how we choose to respond to or remember our experiences is our own, and submodalities are one part of the process. In other words, what happens to us may be beyond our control, but how we respond to or remember it is entirely up to us.

Here is a list of some of the submodalities (or categories of description) possible for each of the five senses:

Visual

- associated/dissociated: seen through our own eyes (associated) or seeing ourselves from the outside (dissociated)
- distance: how far away is the image?
- colour: is the image in full colour, partially coloured or in black and white?
- clarity: is the image clear and focused or blurred?
- location: to the left, to the right, up or down?
- movement: is the image like a film or is it like a photo?
- size: how small or large is the picture?
- duration: how long does the image last?
- frame/panorama: what is your angle or perspective?
- brightness: is the image normal, brighter or dimmer than normal?
- depth: is the image two – or three – dimensional?
- speed: are the movements faster or slower than normal?

Hearing (auditory)

- volume: is the sound soft or loud?
- distance: how far away is the sound?
- location: where is the sound coming from?

- words/sounds: are there either or both?
- speed: is the sound slower or faster than normal?
- clarity: is the sound dull or clear?
- tone: is the sound high or low, hard or soft?
- stereo: is it mono/stereo or moving between the two?
- whose voice it is: your own or someone else's?
- duration: how long does the sound last?
- continuous: is the sound continuous or interrupted?

Feelings

In NLP 'feelings' include internal feelings, emotions, tactile sensations and muscular responses.

- location: where, precisely, do you feel it?
- size: how large or small is the feeling?
- pressure: is the feeling hard, soft or somewhere in between?
- shape: what shape is the feeling?
- intensity: is it strong or weak?
- duration: how long does it last?
- temperature: is it hot or cold?
- frequency: how often do you feel it?
- movement: does it move location at any point?
- texture: is it rough or smooth?
- muscular responses: how are your muscles feeling?

Smell (olfactory) and Taste (gustatory)

Smell and taste play a lesser role and we therefore have fewer submodalities to describe them. Ask yourself these questions about a smell or taste:

- is it pleasant or unpleasant?
- is it strong or weak?
- is it sweet, sour or bitter?
- is it fresh or stale?
- what does it smell/taste like?
- what does the smell/taste remind you of?

The exercises below use submodalities to help build on what works to improve sports performance. When you are finding out about submodalities it is important that the sportsperson is experiencing the situation as near as possible to how it was at the time. It can be helpful (for both parties) to work with someone else, e.g. a coach, team-mate or friends. It is also helpful to write down the submodalities on a piece of paper.

Activity

- Choose a positive sporting experience.
- Relive (access) the experience (state).
- Work through the submodalities checklist, answering all the questions and making a note of the answers.
- Now choose a negative sporting experience.
- Relive (access) the experience (state).
- Work through the submodalities checklist, answering all the questions and making a note of the answers.
- Compare the submodalities of the positive experience with those of the negative experience. How are they different?

Activity

This activity builds on the last Activity and then uses it to change the structure of the actual experience.

- Establish a topic to work on, e.g. motivation.
- Think of a time when you were really motivated, and access that state.
- Find out all the submodalities of the motivated state.
- Break the state by moving around, doing something else for a short while or thinking of something else.
- Think back to a time when you were *not* motivated, and access that state.
- Find out all the submodalities of the unmotivated state.
- Now find two or three important submodality differences between the motivated state and the unmotivated state.
- Change the three submodalities of the unmotivated state into those of the motivated state.
- Notice what differences this makes.

Activity

- Build positive submodalities into your preparation, visualisation and mental rehearsal techniques.

Chapter 16

Use Visualisation And Imagery

Of all aspects of NLP that have entered the wider public domain, the use of visualisation and imagery are among the best known. NLP does not of course claim to have discovered visualisation and imagery, but it has given them a structure and shown how and why they work.

One reason why they work so effectively is that the brain uses imagery as its own internal language. In fact, often the brain does not know the difference between a real event and a really vivid visualisation of it. For example, imagine that you are sucking a juicy lemon right now. Notice how your body responds even though your brain has only imagined it.

Being able to work mentally with images of a good performance, i.e. getting it right inside the head, either before, during or after an event, is a vital skill. In fact, Hall, Rodgers, and Barr (1990) have found that at higher levels of competition more athletes use visualisation and imagery.

> *You need to paint pictures both for yourself and other people.*
>
> Kevin Keegan

Any effective visualisation will include and evoke the appropriate sound, feelings (including tactile sensations, muscular movement, and emotions), smells and taste.

Another obvious but key issue is that it is vital that the visualisation and imagery processes are applied to strengths and/or skills to work on. It is not helpful to have a series of pictures of failures and poor performances inside your head, repeated ad nauseam every time fatigue or weakness take over. Using the technique of visualisation properly actually allows the body to achieve its end goal, without actually having to carry out the process. In other words, it is possible to change and affect the body purely by the power of the mind. Recent evidence from techniques such as biofeedback show how bodily functions such as heart rate, blood pressure, temperature and reaction to pain can all be affected and controlled by the mind, even though for many years these functions were thought to be carried out automatically by the body.

Another useful benefit that visualisation and imagery have is that they allow the mind and body to learn at a much faster rate than just carrying out physical practice for a few hours a day. The potential for this is enormous. It means that practice becomes, if appropriate, something that can be carried out whenever and wherever it is useful.

Visualisation activities can be practised until they become second nature. It is best always to relax fully before you visualise, and to have a clear outcome for the visualisation.

Activity

- Choose a particular skill or ability to work on.
- Where possible, picture the place where the event will take place. If you are unfamiliar with the venue, simply imagine it.
- Keep your mind in the present, avoiding drifting into the past or away into a different event. Keep alert with everything in a clear focus.
- Employ all your five senses. This will heighten the value of the whole experience. Concentrate!
- Make sure that the process is also creating a kinaesthetic response. This is a vital part of ensuring that maximum benefits are achieved.
- Do the visualisation and imagery in an associated state i.e. through your own eyes (in sports psychology this is called internal imagery).
- Make the image as correct and perfect as possible. Help your mind and body to recognise, accept and respond to the highest levels of performance possible. This is part of pre-programming for the future.
- Ensure that everything in your visualisation is happening at normal speed. Sometimes it is possible to lose a sense of time when visualising and imaging. Therefore if the process is about running a hundred metres or putting on a golf green, keep it in real time.

Practise visualising regularly, for a few minutes at a time, at least six times a day for a period of at least four weeks. Turn it into a habitual, unconscious process. Have fun doing it. It doesn't have to be desperately serious. If it is fun it will work for you and help to ensure that you carry on with it. Measure your progress on the field of play. This is where the true results and progress will be shown.

Chapter 17

Develop A Clear Focus

All sportspeople know the value of focusing the mind. Indeed, without that focus, winning would be elusive.

When we are focusing in the here and now we are still absorbing a huge amount of information unconsciously, e.g. the feel of any equipment we are using, what is happening with an opponent, the physical aspects of our performance, the feelings that are attached to the performance, etc. It is important to be able to maintain our focus in the here and now without allowing our minds to drift. If we can learn to become aware of when our minds are drifting, we can then learn how to refocus our minds on the present.

> *Before a big International I liked to sit quietly in a corner and read the programme. Other people did things differently, but it worked well for me. I then knew what I'd got to do. I was ready.*
>
> Dean Richards

As a spectator it is possible to see many sportspeople ensure that their attention is focused in the present. Tim Henman does it by bouncing the ball and looking up before serving and Joel Stransky prepares for an important goal kick by choosing a spot to aim at.

Allowing attentional focus to drift will almost certainly result in a loss of performance. These activities are designed to help focus on the here and now, the present.

Activity – During a Performance or Event

- Develop a visual ritual and anchor for any specific skill required, e.g. taking a penalty, putting, taking guard.

Activity

- Practise narrowing your focus of attention at key moments.

Activity

- Practise focusing only on what is important and tuning out anything that is irrelevant.

Activity

- Have an attention spot to focus on during any pauses in play.

Activity

- Practise making your focus of attention your body, or a particular part of it.

Activity

- Practise developing a focus on your rhythm and balance.

Activity

- Combine your visual focus with an auditory message, e.g. 'stay loose', 'hold the putter correctly', 'hands together' etc.

Chapter 18

Use Your Whole Brain

A good balance between pre-planned activities and 'on the spot' reactive thinking is a major factor in sporting success. Anyone who follows their particular sport in the media will be aware of the sportspeople who are labelled as mavericks because they seem to do whatever comes into their heads, irrespective of the consequences. Equally, successive England teams at rugby, football and cricket have been accused of being dull and boring because they stick rigidly to the tried and tested and are reluctant to take risks.

Part of the reason for the differences between the two approaches is, as ever, down to natural ability. There are those who can only follow the rules and those who always seem to go their own way, sometimes to the annoyance of their team-mates. Natural ability, however, is not the only contributing factor. It is not always the most gifted player who breaks the rules or the least talented who follows them. Many great sportspeople play conventionally a lot of the time, but then are able to do something spontaneous or innovative at the right time, or create a piece of magic that totally changes a game.

Part of the reason for this is the way our brains function. In broad terms, the two halves of our brains function differently.

The left side tends to deal with:

- logic
- calculations
- step-by-step processes
- reason

The right side tends to deal with:

- creativity
- hunches
- intuition

The situation is a little more complex than this, as for example the intuition that the right side of the brain uses is based upon the logic that the left side has developed. The two sides need each other to achieve an appropriate balance.

To provide a more detailed picture, the left side of the brain:

- takes things in sequentially
- sees and likes a step-by-step approach
- likes language, placing a lot of emphasis on words
- likes to use logic
- covers every aspect
- tends to be aware of time
- likes to set and work towards goals
- likes to carry out reviews
- will often over-analyse information
- can become withdrawn or obstinate

The right side of the brain:

- prefers to do everything at once
- sees the big or whole picture
- will use and rely on instinct
- gets bored with too much detail
- is not too bothered about time
- likes to work with pictures and images
- prefers general rather than specific goals
- 'daydreams' or seems to wander
- is very aware of spatial perception

Another vital factor for the sportsperson to be aware of is that:

- the left side of the brain controls the right side of the body
- the right side of the brain controls the left side of the body

When training or practising it is important to design activities that utilise both sides of the brain. This not only ensures that there is something that appeals to everyone, but also that key skills can be developed. Many sportspeople tend to develop comfortable routines which become conditioned responses. In other words, given a particular situation, they are likely to respond in a particular way. There is nothing necessarily wrong with this (in fact it can have many strengths) but it can also have limitations, as it means that the response is predictable, e.g. always placing a penalty kick on the same side, always bowling a bouncer after being hit for four, always doing the same thing with a second serve. Using instinct to do something completely unexpected can often throw an opponent off form.

Brain Gym, developed by Dr Paul Dennison and Gail Dennison (see bibliography for details) focuses on exercising both sides of the brain to bring about greater harmony. In addition, many techniques in NLP have the effect of developing both sides of the brain. Techniques that work particularly well are mind-mapping, flow-charts, mnemonics and brain-storming.

Activity

Develop broader skills by:

- playing other sports that involve both sides of the brain, e.g. basketball, football, tennis
- practising balancing on a beam, or something narrow
- doing a different physical-and-mental skill e.g. dancing, playing an instrument or singing
- developing a creative hobby, e.g. painting, pottery
- doing sports/activities that involve the whole body, e.g. swimming, skiing

Activity

Left-brain sportspeople who want to develop a more balanced right-brain approach can try:

- brain-storming
- visualising
- listening to your hunches – and acting on them
- doing things in different ways
- taking up a creative hobby
- tuning in to your emotions and feelings
- paying attention to your body rhythm
- trying something spontaneous when playing sports

Activity

Right-brain sports people who want to develop a more balanced left-brain approach can try:

- planning an activity in detail
- doing things in sequence
- making a 'to do list' – and sticking to it
- listening for details in conversation
- analysing decisions
- using logic
- when facing a big decision, developing a list of plusses and minuses
- paying attention to holding your sports equipment properly
- paying attention to your body movements

Chapter 19

Use Ritual And Habits

All sportspeople have developed some rituals and habits and some have taken them further and allowed them to develop into superstitions. Rituals and superstitions are not the same thing. Superstitions are props built upon fears or a previous good performance, e.g. a lucky shirt or a lucky piece of equipment.

Positive superstitions – those based on a previous good performance can have a useful role to play. The odd thing is that when a positive superstition fails to produce the goods, the belief that lies behind the superstition often remains unquestioned. The superstition is perpetuated, *in spite of the evidence.* This is yet another example of the power of beliefs and of the individuality of every person's truth.

I'm not really a believer in superstitions.
I just got myself right inside myself before a game.
Kevin Keegan

Rituals and habits may be used to regain concentration, peak for a specific moment or to relax. They send a signal to the brain that a specific response is required. In this sense they are like the anchors we use in NLP, triggers used to create a response.

When watching professional sportspeople, either live or on TV, it is worth watching out for their rituals and habits, e.g. Allan Donald standing at this end of his run-up, gathering himself, David Seaman's process when someone is taking a penalty against him, or Rob Andrew or Joel Stransky about to take a penalty kick in rugby.

Some of these rituals may have been developed deliberately, but many of them are developed unconsciously. We use them again and again because they work, even though we may not be aware of what we are doing or why. Some rituals may have been developed deliberately but have since become habits that we are no longer aware of.

All the sportspeople interviewed for this book reported having rituals and habits of some sort or another. At the beginning of the interview many said they did not have rituals or if they did it was only one or two. During the interview, however, it became apparent that they normally have many more, and that they use them in particular ways. Most of them have different rituals and habits for different parts of the performance. For example Ivan Lendl, the tennis player, always used to bounce the ball a prescribed number of times before a big serve, and Stephen Hendry goes through the same routine when a break has gone awry, to get his concentration back and clear his mind.

> *I had two mental nets before each innings.*
> Darren Maddy, Leicestershire Cricketer,
> quoted in the *Leicester Mercury*

Rituals and habits might be a word, a gesture, an action or any signal that has been rehearsed and practised, e.g. the squash player touching the wall, the cricketer taking guard again or touching his cap, the team huddle, the golfer lining up a putt. A particularly dramatic ritual shown in the 'Living With the Lions' video shows the forwards on the 1997 tour of South Africa going through their rituals (while one of the backs can be heard throwing up off camera!).

Some of the benefits of rituals and habits are:

- clarifying goals (either individual or team)
- focusing attention
- psyching up
- distracting attention
- instant relaxation
- tuning into (or avoiding) external noise
- concentrating on a specific skill
- concentrating on a specific moment
- focusing attention on a particular part of the body
- focusing attention on a particular piece of equipment
- creating or maintaining attention in the here and now
- staying calm

To use rituals and habits effectively practise them regularly, at least as much as any physical practice. Relying on them to work on the day without practice is not a good idea.

The key elements in rituals and habits are that they narrow the focus of attention and heighten concentration, ready for the key moment. This helps in not allowing distractions and interference factors in. Watch a number of professional golfers lining up an important putt. Superficially they all look as though they are doing the same thing. Closer attention will reveal that, although the end objective is the same thing, i.e. holing the putt, different things are happening. Each of them is gauging distance, inspecting the green etc., but each is also doing something different either physically or mentally.

Some key principles for rituals and habits are:

- keep them short and simple
- use ones directly under your control
- practise them day to day
- have special ones for the extra big occasion
- don't let your opponent know what your rituals and habits are
- for pre-performance rituals and habits, focus on the internal signals
- during performance, expand rituals and habits to include both internal and external cues
- ensure that rituals and habits include kinaesthetic elements, i.e. feelings, emotions, muscle and tactile sensations
- pay particular attention to the feedback you receive kinaesthetically; work on 'feeling good' and 'feeling right'

Imagine a cricketer who has been beaten by the first five balls in an over. Worse than that, he knows that he hasn't a clue about why it has been happening or what to do about it. If he allows these thoughts to continue it is likely he will not survive the sixth ball. A ritual will allow him to clear his mind and focus on the next ball rather than the last five. His chances of success then become much higher.

Focusing attention is one of the key functions of rituals and habits. Many studies have been carried out into the factors that make certain sportspeople stand out and excel. Always, near the top of the list is the ability to get themselves together for the big throw, the important putt or whatever the key moment is. Rituals and habits undoubtedly contribute to this ability.

The purpose of pre-performance rituals and habits is to pull the attention together and focus it, and to avoid being distracted by either internal or external interference factors.

During the performance itself it is obviously important that the same things occur, but there are likely to be many more potential interference factors, e.g. your opponent(s), the crowd, the referee or umpire, your team-mates. In addition, the game itself must be played. It is very easy to get flooded by information and then lose focus and concentration.

To counteract this it is important to concentrate on 'own' performance rather than too much on the opponent. For example, in a football match, if you are expecting a hard time from a particular opponent, and they beat you the first three or four times, it is very easy to start concentrating on them rather than the key issue, which is what *you* can control i.e. your own response and performance.

Rituals and habits play a small, but important part in controlling the situation. There may be some more fundamental issues to deal with, e.g. lack of belief, insecurity about maintaining a place in the team, pressure from team-mates, etc. Rituals and habits will create the opportunity to reveal and tackle these issues.

Activity

- Decide on a key moment in your sport when a ritual would help.
- Choose an appropriate ritual or habit, e.g. touching the peak of a cap for a cricketer, preparing for a place kick for a rugby player, checking instruments for a car driver, bouncing of the ball for a tennis player.
- Operate the ritual whenever you need to.
- Practise it outside the real game.
- Review its effectiveness and appropriateness regularly.
- Make your ritual look natural and spontaneous to the observer.

This last point can be quite important when dealing with an opponent. For example, all the books written by professional poker players comment on how their opponents reveal their true intentions by a gesture, mannerism, word or reaction. We are all aware to some extent of how to 'read' our partners or children in a similar way. NLP can help us to harness and develop this skill to our advantage.

Activity

Rituals and habits are forms of anchors, therefore the process for creating them is similar.

- Identify the resource state you want e.g. total concentration for a putt, calmness when taking a penalty, hanging in at the end of a hard game.
- Decide what ritual or habit you will use to access that state. Use as many of the five senses as possible.
- Mentally rehearse the specific moment when you will use the ritual or habit.
- Develop and recognise the response you achieve both mentally and physically when using the ritual or habit (even if practising it in your armchair).
- Use the ritual or habit during normal training and review the results.
- Introduce it into normal play.
- Review the results regularly.

Chapter 20

Create And Use Body-awareness

It would appear obvious to most people that all sportspeople should have really good body-awareness, and of course many have. However, it is odd how many seem not to. Also it is strange how many clubs, managers and coaches do not include some body-awareness training as part of normal practice.

One reason may be that it is often viewed (incorrectly) as something that we either have or have not, rather than as something that can be developed. Body-awareness can help us to identify any problems that may develop into injuries, before they have the chance to do so.

Various people loosely connected with NLP have developed physical exercise methodologies. Among the best known are Feldenkrais and Rolfe. In addition, many sportspeople use either Pilates or the Alexander technique. Each of these can be learnt through specialist trainers and all of them create a valuable sense of body-awareness. In addition, they are also useful for physically preparing for sport, warming down from it, or aiding improvement from injury.

Based upon NLP principles, the following well-known activity can be used to create and use body-awareness.

Activity

- Lie down and relax fully, with your eyes shut.
- Pay attention to your feet and ankles. Does your left foot feel different to your right? If so, in what way? Pay close attention to the different feelings between the toes. How are they different? Do your two ankles feel different? What about differences in weight, warmth, tension, tightness, looseness, etc.?
- Now pay attention to your lower legs. Think about the same questions.
- Do the same for your upper legs, including your groin and backside.
- Repeat for your lower stomach.
- Repeat for your chest.
- Repeat for your back.
- Repeat for your hands and wrists.
- Repeat for your lower arms and elbows.
- Repeat for your upper arms and shoulders.
- Repeat for your neck.
- Repeat for your jaw.
- Repeat for your nose, ears and eyes.
- Repeat for your forehead and the top of your head.
- Take a final few minutes to go back through each part of the body. If anything seems strange or gives intriguing information, pay some attention to it (remember you are *not* trying to change anything, simply becoming more aware of it).
- Having completed the profile, gradually return your attention to the room and your surroundings.

Practise becoming aware of particular parts of your body while actually practising or training, e.g. when standing at the non-striker's end while playing cricket, while warming up, while walking from one hole to another in golf, while preparing for a line-out in rugby.

Chapter 21

Harness Aggression

Everyone who has played or watched sport will have seen (or carried out) acts of aggression. Quite often these are spur-of-the-moment responses to a real or imagined injustice, e.g. an unfair tackle from an opponent, a bad decision from the referee or umpire. Sometimes they are prompted by our response to a mistake of our own.

Very few sportspeople have not at some point reacted in the heat of the moment and then regretted it later. Some of these incidents have become legendary, e.g. Paul Gascoigne's tackle in the 1991 Cup Final, Courtney Walsh's bowling against the English tail-enders in the Jamaica Test Match and David Beckham's response in the England v Argentina World Cup game. One of the factors that brings extreme pressure to bear, and then exploits it, is media attention. People who are not even football fans will have seen the David Beckham incident reported in the press, watched it from every angle on TV, heard it commented on by every pundit. Obviously there is nothing wrong with this. It is right and proper that misdemeanours should be picked up on and punished. The issue is that the pressure to succeed is partially developed by the media, and once an aggressive act has taken place, it sometimes becomes bigger than the game itself. This creates an ongoing cycle of pressure to succeed, and to 'live down' the incident. Unfortunately, the greater the pressure, the more likely it is to spill over into aggression.

There are various models used in sports psychology regarding aggression. Richard H. Cox in his book *Sports Psychology, Concepts And Applications* uses the following table to explain the three most noted theories of aggression:

Theory	Basic Tenets Of Theory
Instinct Theory	1. Aggression is an innate biological drive. 2. Aggression results in purging or venting of pent up emotions. 3. Sport provides a safe and socially acceptable outlet for aggression.
Frustration – Aggression Hypothesis	1. Aggression is a natural consequence of frustration. 2. The strength of the tendency to aggression is related to the strength, degree and number of frustrations. 3. Overt aggression acts as a catharsis or release against further aggression.
Social Learning Theory	1. The need for aggression is a learned response. 2. Aggression begets further aggression. 3. Aggression does not serve as a vent or catharsis against further aggression.

Whichever of these theories we choose to accept, it is clear that aggression has always played a role in sport, and will continue to do so. The key lies in learning to use aggression purposefully.

Two specific NLP tools that can assist in harnessing aggression are **perceptual positions** and **internal dialogue**.

There are three perceptual positions:

First Position
We are in first position when we are looking at things from our own point of view only.

Second Position
We are in second position when we are able to look at things from another person's point of view.

Third Position
We are in third position when we are playing the role of a detached observer, observing ourselves and others. We are usually in third position when we are reviewing a game or match after the event.

It is in first position that we are most likely to use aggression inappropriately. If we can move into second position and experience the other person's point of view, this is less likely to happen. From third position we can observe all the players involved and, from a more detached, less emotional viewpoint, give ourselves guidance as to how to respond.

Activity

- Think about a recent sporting experience where you became aggressive. Associate fully into the experience.
- Now place the experience up on a stage or screen. Place yourself in the audience watching yourself on the stage or screen (you are now in third position).
- While watching yourself get aggressive, decide on a piece of advice that would help the you on the stage or screen to harness the aggression.
- From third position offer the advice to the you in first position. Allow the first-position you to receive the advice and respond to it.

This simple activity is already used by many people in all walks of life to develop the habit of 'self- coaching'.

Self-talk (or internal dialogue) is the voice we hear inside our head. No one else ever hears this voice or the conversation it creates. Some people call it their 'conscience', which in itself is a revealing phrase as it implies that it is used in a negative way, i.e. to discourage us, de-motivate us, tell us what *not* to do. According to some psychologists, about 70% of internal self-talk can be negative.

Self-talk is an important factor in aggression, as we respond to the voice in our head (e.g. 'That's not fair!' or 'Go get him!') or use it after the event to justify what we did. The more our internal dialogue justifies inappropriate aggression, the more likely we are to repeat it.

You keep responsibility for yourself.
Everybody is emotional but you make it work for you.
Kevin Keegan

Activity

- Practise paying more attention to your internal dialogue. Listen for messages that trigger aggression, and notice how you respond.
- In order to break the pattern of using self-talk to create or condone aggression, substitute any negative dialogue *immediately* with a more positive message.

Chapter 22

Utilise The Crowd

Many sportspeople, whether professional or amateur, see the crowd as a source of major concern and difficulty. This is a perfectly understandable reaction, as the crowd has become a major factor. The football team playing in front of their own fans, the boxer fighting in his home town, Tim Henman playing at Wimbledon, the French football team winning the World Cup in their own country, are all examples of this.

The campaign against David Beckham since the World Cup is an interesting example of the extent fans will go to in order to make a point. All the evidence indicates that as well as making a point about England's exit from the competition, the fans also saw it as an opportunity to potentially put him off his game when playing against their club. In fact, pre-season media reports suggested it could go as far as forcing him to have to move clubs and play his football in Europe. His performances on the pitch at the start of the 1998/9 season soon quietened down this speculation.

One of the complications regarding the crowd is that it is not always quite as simple as playing at home being helpful and playing away being negative. For example, in the 1997/98 football season, Crystal Palace became known for their inability to win at home. Many sportspeople actually prefer to play away as the crowd expectation is different and it provides them with fewer distractions.

To be really successful, it is vital to be able to perform to our highest capability, wherever we are playing. This includes the fun squash player, who, when playing at the local leisure centre, loses whenever someone is watching, and the professional playing in front of thousands of people.

The crowd are really important. Sometimes they love you, sometimes they don't, but they always know if you're being honest.

Kevin Keegan

Some sportspeople are able to raise their game for the big occasion and the big crowd. Bill Beaumont talks about Gordon Brown, the Scottish rugby player, doing this, and David Gower was an example of someone who tended to perform at a higher level in front of a large audience, rather than in a virtually deserted county ground. Some commentators (and sportspeople themselves) believe that this is the one factor that separates the truly great from the very good.

The crowd is such a large factor in the big occasion that the ability to utilise it effectively is a major advantage. When sportspeople start out with their new sport, the presence of a crowd can be a limiting factor and the fear of looking foolish in front of others inhibits the development of ability and prowess. This fear actually applies at all levels of sport, from the beginner to the Wimbledon tennis player afraid of serving a double fault, or to the footballer taking a penalty in the World Cup finals.

The combination of having a crowd and dealing with its expectations is a complex one for the sportsperson, whether playing individually or in a team. A study by Varca (1980) suggests that aggression is a key factor; the home team tends to be more 'functionally aggressive' whereas the away team is more 'dysfunctionally aggressive'. In other words, home teams tend to focus more on responses that encourage higher performance, while away teams are more niggly, argue more with officials, and commit more faults.

It is therefore vital for the away team or player to be aware of this tendency and turn it around with an appropriate plan. This plan might include the following factors:

- focusing on careful defence
- tactics for appropriate attack
- ways of dealing with the crowd
- calming measures
- avoiding arguments
- not committing misdemeanours
- focusing on specific performance issues
- focusing on specific outcomes

The activities below will help with formulating this plan.

Activity

- Practise using the perceptual position techniques covered in chapter 21, ***Harness Aggression***. This will help you to detach yourself from anything negative going on.

Activity

- Before the start of play, mentally rehearse being the total centre of attention *and enjoy every second of it*.
- Do this initially in a dissociated state so that you can change anything that doesn't look, sound, feel, smell or taste right.
- Then step inside and become *fully* associated. Be aware of every piece of feedback your senses are providing.

Activity

- Develop rituals and habits to either limit the effect of the audience and the environment or, more purposefully, to create more empowering beliefs about your performance. Rituals and habits are covered in chapter 19.

Chapter 23

Achieve Consistent Levels Of Motivation

Giving value for money was a big issue for me. This motivated me no matter where I was playing.
Kevin Keegan

Motivation is a complex issue. Answering the questions below will help you to become more aware of your own levels of motivation as well as the many factors involved.

- Do you use positive or negative words in your conversations and your internal dialogue (examples of positive words are 'will' and 'can', while 'must' and 'should' are negative words)?
- Do you focus on the positive or the negative aspect of your performance?
- Do you look forward in a calm manner to a forthcoming event, or do you get over-aroused or under-aroused?
- Do you have clear goals for both playing the match and winning?
- Do your thoughts become more positive or negative as the event draws near?
- Do you deal with poor performance in an honest, realistic way without dwelling on it for too long?
- Do you have both short-term and long-term goals to improve your sports performance?
- Do you know *why* these are so important to you?
- Do you take responsibility for your levels of motivation rather than blaming other factors if something doesn't completely work out?
- Do you focus on the future or the past?
- What words do other people use about your levels of motivation? How do you react to this?
- Do you allow yourself to be as good as it is possible for you to be?
- Which of the following four motivation states best describes you?

1. I am able to deal with any challenges that appear. I remain poised, focused and in control. I am happy with my response and performance, knowing that I give totally my best.

2. I am driven by the need to prove something by how I perform. I feel I must win because I want to avoid looking stupid or bad. I want all the rewards that go with winning. Sometimes I focus on the past, sometimes on the future.

3. I don't really feel bothered at the moment, although I have been before and will be again later. I don't focus on the here and now.

4. I feel the pressure of other people's expectations. They are over-emphasising the importance of winning. I wish they would just leave me alone. I feel burnt out.

> *I'm very lucky in the motivation department. I don't have to get motivated to give my best because if I've eaten the right foods, got the right attitude, had a good night's sleep, done the preparation, the equipment is OK, then I've been getting myself motivated without even realising it.*
>
> Shaun Tacey, Speedway Rider

Having answered these questions, you should have a clearer idea of any problem areas in your motivation. The activities below will help you to tackle these effectively.

Activity

- Repeat the exercise on moving from an unmotivated state to a motivated state. This appears in chapter 15, ***Pay Attention To What Works***.

A well-known NLP technique is called 'Wishing to Wanting'. Its purpose is to establish the difference for an individual between what it feels like to wish for something and what it feels like to want something, and then to make a wish become a want (evidence suggests that our wishes remain wishes, whereas we tend to actually achieve what we want).

Activity

- Remind yourself about submodalities by re-reading chapter 15, ***Pay Attention To What Works.***
- Choose something in your sport that is a 'wish' for you.
- Step into that state of wishing.
- Find out all the submodalities of the state and make a note of them.
- Break state by thinking about something else or doing something else for a few seconds.
- Now choose something in your sport that is a 'want' for you.
- Step into that state of wanting.
- Find out all the submodalities of the state and make a note of them.
- Break state by thinking about something else or doing something else for a few seconds.
- Look carefully at your lists of 'wish' submodalities and 'want' submodalities. Choose two major differences.
- Now go back into the experience of the 'wish' state. Change those two submodalities so that they are the same as in your 'want' state.
- Notice the difference that this makes to your motivation to achieve the 'wish'.

Section Four

Coaching Yourself

Chapter 24

Manage Stress And Burnout

In a sporting context, the impact of stress can be enormous. The combination of press interest, pressure to maintain or improve our levels of performance or maintain our place in the team can lead to all the classic symptoms of stress.

According to Dr Teresa Foot, Ph.D, these symptoms may include:

- tension headaches
- low back pain or tension in your neck and shoulder muscles
- feeling sick for no obvious reason
- rapid or irregular heart-beat
- loss of appetite, or eating for comfort when you are not hungry
- frequent indigestion or gut disorders
- trembling hands
- having hot or cold spells for no reason
- twitching limbs in bed at night
- extreme irritability
- losing your ability to laugh, or feeling depressed
- no longer caring about life or people
- loss of libido
- feeling uptight or anxious most of the time
- feeling hopeless about the future
- being tearful
- uncontrollable outbursts of temper
- feeling under pressure all the time

Most of us know that *some* stress is essential to peak performance. The diagram below illustrates the classic model of this relationship between stress and performance:

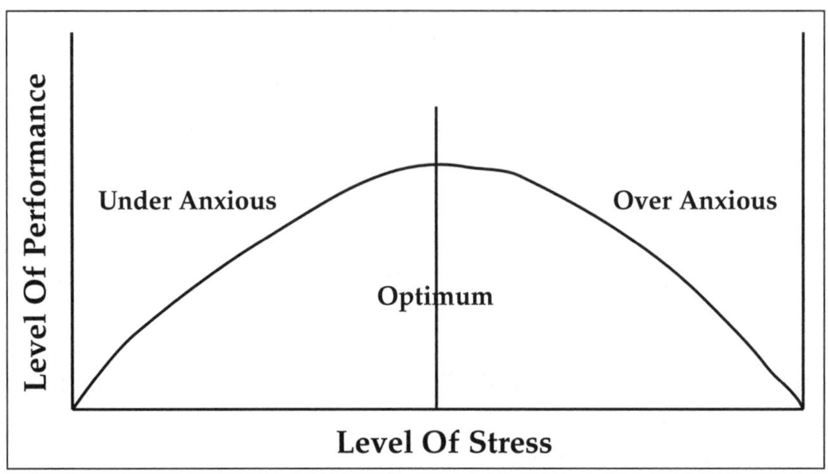

Although this model applies to all of us, the actual amount of stress required to overload each of us is highly individual. There is not a pre-set amount that causes overload. In fact, we all know people who seem to be able to manage massive amounts of stress and others who are blown away by the first sight of a problem. Too much stress – either physical or psychological – can lead to the phenomenon of burnout.

In his book *Sports Slump Busting,* Alan S Goldberg offers the following questionnaire to establish your level of burnout.

Answer True or False to the following questions:

- I am tired all the time.
- I don't enjoy practice the way I used to.
- When I practise I frequently wish I were somewhere else.
- I dread competing.
- It has been a long time since I've really had fun competing.
- I continually question why I remain in the sport.
- I find it hard to keep focused on my goals.
- I seem to get injured more than ever before.
- My injuries never seems to heal.
- My attitude seems to have become worse over the past several months.
- I resent having to sacrifice so much of my time for the sport.
- I don't handle the discomfort from hard training as well as I did last year.

- Sometimes I don't even care that I don't care.
- I'm more negative than usual about my training and myself.
- I have trouble concentrating in practice.
- I put myself down a lot lately.
- I really resent my coach.
- I have more trouble getting along with team-mates than ever before.
- I feel pressurised by others to remain in the sport.
- I don't seem able to bounce back from setbacks like I used to.

Give yourself one point for each time you have answered 'true', then add up the total number of points. If you scored between 1 and 3 out of a possible 20 points, then you probably don't need to be concerned about burnout. Scores between 4 and 7 indicate that you are starting to 'cook' and you could use some time off. Scores between 8 and 14 indicate that you are in desperate need of a vacation from training and competition. If you scored 15 or higher, then you are seriously burned out and need to sit down with your coach and have a heart-to-heart discussion.

One problem with questionnaires like this is that a lot of the answers are not either true or false but somewhere in between. Some of us may view all of these features of burnout as 'normal' to some degree or at any particular time.

The problem is that a situation, if left, may incrementally, or suddenly, get worse and then precipitate a crisis. Because whatever is going wrong is not getting any better, some of us may compensate with physical training rather than sorting out the mental aspects. Another response may be to 'shut down', to be there physically, but actually be only be going through the motions. Both of these responses are likely to result in more injuries, and there is the danger that the burnout will intensify, inappropriate responses to it will intensify, and the pattern will repeat itself again and again.

The key is to avoid doing more of what is already contributing to the problem, and to turn the negative situation into a positive one.

The people who cope with stress and burnout effectively all seem to have a sense of:

- commitment
- control
- challenge
- balance/realism

It may be useful to bear these features in mind while working through the activities that follow.

Activity

Create a clearer picture of both the problem and the solution by answering these questions:

- What's wrong?
- Why do I have this problem?
- How long have I had it?
- How does it limit me?
- Why does this problem stop me from doing what I want to do?
- Whose fault is this problem?
- When was the worst time that I experienced this problem?
- What do I want?
- When do I want it?
- How will I know when I have it?
- When I get what I want, what else might improve?
- When I get what I want, is there anything I may lose?
- What resources do I have available to help me to get what I want?
- How best can I utilise these resources?
- What am I going to start doing *now* to get what I want?

Activity

Learn to understand yourself better by:

- becoming more self-aware
- noticing the state of your body
- noticing your thought patterns
- acknowledging the factors from your past that are influencing you today

Activity

Take control by:

- dealing more effectively with situations and people
- taking responsibility for your own actions and feeling
- balancing your needs with those of others
- tackling issues that need to be dealt with

Activity

Develop your physical resilience by:

- getting healthy with a good diet and no smoking
- learning to relax
- getting regular (and varied) exercise
- taking breaks

Activity

Develop your psychological resilience by:

- recognising your own mental stress triggers
- being social and enjoying the support of other people
- focusing on future goals instead of past mistakes
- challenging your own negative thinking and self-talk
- laughing a lot

Activity

Deal with practical issues by:

- reviewing your environment and your lifestyle
- recognising your ability to make tough choices
- creating a balanced lifestyle

Activity

- Remind yourself about submodalities by re-reading chapter 15, ***Pay Attention To What Works***.
- Think back to a sports situation when you were over-stressed.
- Step into that state and access it fully.
- Find out all the submodalities of the state and make a note of them.
- Break state by thinking about something else or doing something else for a few seconds.
- Now think back to a sports situation when you were free of negative stress.
- Step into that state and access it fully.
- Find out all the submodalities of the state and make a note of them.
- Break state by thinking about something else or doing something else for a few seconds.
- Compare your lists of submodalities for the two states, and select two or three that seem most important.
- Go back into your over-stressed state and change those two or three submodalities by substituting them with those of your un-stressed state.
- Notice what difference this makes to your level of negative stress. Experiment with changing other submodalities if you like.
- End this activity by using one of the relaxation techniques from the next chapter (never leave yourself in a stressed state).

In addition to these activities, the activities in the next section on relaxation can help to counteract stress.

Chapter 25

Use Relaxation Techniques

In order to maintain and improve our performance, it is vital that we are able to switch off and recharge our batteries. Fortunately there are many effective ways to achieve this, two of which are autogenic training and hypnosis.

Autogenic Training

Autogenic training consists of a series of six mental exercises that help us to calm our minds by switching off the body's natural 'fight or flight' responses. This allows us to relax deeply, and it has the added benefit of stimulating the body's power to heal itself.

Autogenic training has been used successfully to tackle issues such as high blood pressure, poor concentration, depression, irritable bowel syndrome, palpitations, anxiety, recovery after injury, sleep disorders and ulcers. As it is a structured process, this book is not the place to go into it in any depth. Any sportsperson, manager or coach who wishes to know more should contact:

British Association for Autogenic Training
18 Holtsmere Close
Garston
Watford
Herts WD2 6NG

A good book on the subject is *Autogenic Training* by Dr Kai Kermani, who can also be contacted direct at:

Holistic Health
Healing and Autogenic Centre
10 Connaught Hill
Loughton
Essex 1G10 4DU

Hypnosis

Gold medallist Iwan Thomas last night revealed the bizarre secret behind his stunning 400 metres European Championship triumph – he was hypnotised. 'Without a doubt working with Robert Farago made me mentally prepared for the race and he played a major part in helping me win'.

Daily Mail, August 25th 1998.

Most people's idea of hypnosis is based upon television or live performances, where people are 'made' to behave strangely to entertain an audience. Medicinal or therapeutic hypnosis, which is being increasingly used by mainstream medicine, is very different. Hypnotism has been studied at medical schools in Britain since 1955, and is now generally recognised as a useful part of modern science and medicine.

The key to hypnosis is that it creates an 'altered state' of consciousness. We have all experienced daydreaming, in which we go into a mild trance. Hypnosis takes this trance-state just a little further. Although this state appears to be like sleep, it differs in that we are still able to respond, and our five senses are heightened.

The popular image of having to be 'put under' is not entirely accurate. Many people nowadays use a form of self-hypnosis to help them deal with key issues or improve performance in key areas of their lives. The research indicates that post-hypnotic suggestions are very powerful in breaking up negative habits and establishing more useful, powerful ones in their place. This is obviously very appealing to the sportsperson. They can deal with self-limiting beliefs, anxiety, various forms of phobias. The notion of being in control of, and responsible for self, is a powerful one for anyone who believes in the power of self.

If you would like to explore hypnosis further, speak to your GP or contact:

British Hypnosis Research
212 Piccadilly
London W1V 9LD
Telephone 0171 666 6700

There are many books available on the subject, e.g. *Self Hypnosis: Creating Your Own Destiny* by Henry Leo Bolduc, or *Self Hypnosis: Step by Step* by Dr JP Guyonnaud (full details of both these books appear in the bibliography of this book).

Activity

To relax after a busy day:

- find somewhere warm and quiet
- wear loose clothing in which you feel comfortable
- use a relaxation tape or some soothing music to calm your mind and allow yourself to relax
- practise calm breathing as a method of releasing tension

One of the key factors in relaxation is the ability to breathe deeply and correctly. Whenever we are under stress our breathing pattern is likely to change. For many people this means breathing more shallowly and not getting the right amount of oxygen to the brain. Concentrating on breathing correctly is a good way to induce relaxation. Correct breathing, called 'abdominal breathing', involves breathing deeply – as if into the abdomen – instead of simply using the top part of our lungs (as we do when we are stressed).

Activity

- Get into a comfortable position, preferably sitting rather than lying down.
- For two minutes, carry out deep abdominal breathing, ensuring that you are inhaling to the fullest extent.
- Exhale in short bursts through the left nostril while ensuring that you are pulling in your stomach with each exhalation. Do this for two minutes.
- For a further two minutes, carry out deep abdominal breathing, exhaling naturally.
- Exhale in short bursts through the right nostril for two minutes.
- For a final two minutes, carry out deep abdominal breathing, exhaling naturally.

NOTE: Don't do this activity if you have a background of high blood pressure, strokes, heart disease or epilepsy.

Activity

- Lie down in a warm comfortable place with no distractions.
- Tighten all the muscles in your feet and ankles, holding for about 10 seconds. Be totally aware of the effect of the tension, with all your senses. Then say the word 'relax' to yourself. Relax *slowly,* enjoying the sensations in both your muscles and your mind. Imagine the tenseness flowing out onto or into the surface you are lying on.
- Breathe in deeply, filling the abdomen, then pause, breathe out and enjoy the moment.
- Tighten the muscles from your ankles up to and including your knees, keeping the feet and ankles relaxed. Be aware of all your senses. Then relax slowly, feeling the tension flowing out of your body. Breathe in deeply, then exhale.
- Repeat for the area above the knees up to and including the thighs, groin and backside.
- Repeat for the lower stomach, including the belly button.
- Repeat for your chest area.
- Repeat for your hands and wrists.
- Repeat for your lower arms up to and including your elbows.
- Repeat for your upper arms and shoulders.
- Repeat for your neck.
- Repeat for your jaw.
- Repeat for your nose, eyes and ears.
- Repeat for the top of your head.
- Tense the whole body, using the word 'relax' to signal the release of the tenseness. See hear, feel, smell and taste the feelings of relaxation. Breathe in and out slowly and deeply.

It can be worthwhile to record these instructions using your own voice (or the voice of a loved one). Any of the relaxation activities should be carried out at least once a day for a minimum period of two weeks. You could do this directly after training or, if more privacy is required, in bed last thing at night.

Chapter 26

Create Internal Rewards

A danger for us as sportspeople is that we may go past being prepared and focused and move into being, or becoming, obsessed. There can be a thin dividing line between the two, but most people will recognise the classic signs of obsession, e.g. playing on through an injury, blaming ourselves (or our opponent) for everything, becoming irritable with those closest to us, losing our sense of humour, etc.

There are many reasons why obsessions develop, e.g. inability to relax, a lack of balance in our lives or internal and external pressures. One of the key reasons is our inability to reward ourselves appropriately. No matter what the result or improvement in performance, we beat ourselves up, focus on the negatives and push ourselves even harder. In this mood, even winning can be viewed as failure if the margin was not enough, or the opponent was not defeated by a sufficient degree.

Obviously there are advantages to caring this much and in wanting to win and perform well. However, if we carry it to extremes, we may become so over-aroused that we 'burnout' and cannot give of our best. Alternatively, we may just not be able to peak at the right time and therefore underachieve.

The consequences of either of these is that the right results are not achieved, and a cycle is created where we 'try harder', either in training or in actual performance, and we actually worsen the situation. The reason for this is that mentally (and sometimes physically), we are doing *more of what is not working* and expecting things to improve. The ability to create internal rewards (which may involve others as well) is the key to our sportspeople being able to achieve a balance in our lives and consequently give of our best in our chosen sport.

Make your ability your best friend and never abuse it!

Alan Ball

One of the reasons why we may not be able to reward ourselves is we have allowed ourselves to become focused on the negative, e.g. what is wrong, how difficult it all is, how good everybody else is, etc. This means that we have developed what some people call an 'inappropriate attitude'.

In NLP terms, attitudes are 'invisible', i.e. they cannot be seen. Our attitudes lie deep within us and yet *can affect everything we do*. The odd thing about attitudes is that they are spoken about and analysed all the time. Virtually every interview with a sportsperson, coach or manager includes a reference to an attitude, be it good or bad, and the consequences of it. Even outside sport, at home, school or in business, attitudes are often used to explain everything. Phrases such as 'they have a bad attitude', or 'if you want to succeed you are going to have to change your attitude' are used frequently. Even in personal relationships, attitudes are referred to (often negatively) to explain aspects of another person's behaviour.

Our attitudes (along with our values and beliefs) are vital to our success in all aspects of life, including sport. The fascinating thing is that many people seem to consider them as somehow fixed and unchangeable. The fact that some people do not change their attitudes does not mean that they cannot be changed.

If we have a particular attitude about ourselves, e.g. 'I'm not very good in front of a large crowd',or a particular attitude about an opponent, e.g. 'they're bound to be much better than me', we will filter the actual evidence by generalising one example, distorting evidence to support our attitude or deleting evidence to the contrary. Thus we now have confirmation that our view was right all along.

Taken further this can mean we start to develop phobias about certain opponents or venues, which further embeds our negative attitude and turns it into a self-fulfilling prophecy. One further implication of this can be that in a team sport, our attitude can start to affect other team members. The impact on team morale and performance in these circumstances can be catastrophic.

Of course, a good or positive attitude makes playing the sport fun and challenging, and shows itself in the results achieved. NLP has found that learning and change take place on different levels, as illustrated in Robert Dilts's model:

Logical Level Model

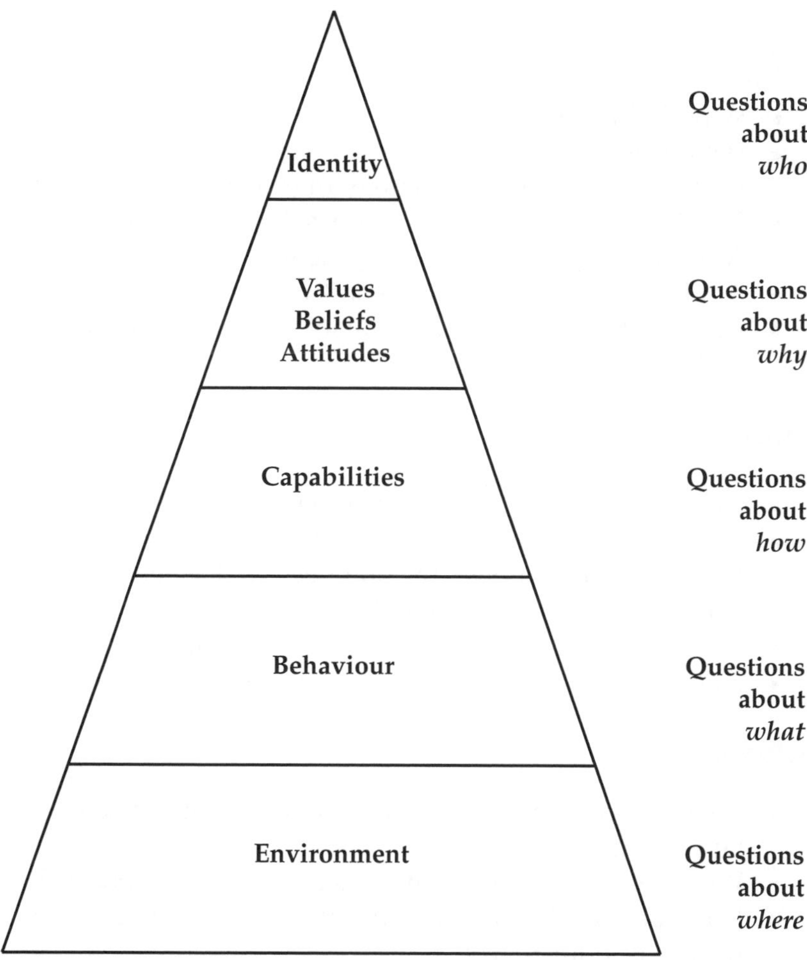

Identity

- Who am I as an individual?
- What do I stand for?
- What makes me unique?
- What is my mission and vision?
- Do I have a personal philosophy?

Beliefs, Values And Attitudes

- Why do I want to change?
- What is my personal style?
- Do I treat myself (and others) with respect and trust?
- Do I live out my beliefs and values, i.e. do 'I walk my talk?'
- Are my beliefs and values congruent?
- Am I consistent in my beliefs and values?
- Do I acknowledge other people's beliefs, values and attitudes?

Capabilities

- How do I need to go about creating change?
- What skills and knowledge do I already have?
- What skills and knowledge do I need to develop?
- Do I manage my own capabilities effectively?
- How do I manage my own levels of motivation?
- How do I manage my own personal leadership?

Behaviour

- What are my current key behaviours – both effective and non-effective?
- Which of my current behaviours do I reward or punish?
- Do I operate a 'carrot' or 'stick' approach to myself, i.e. do I reward or punish myself?
- What new behaviours do I need to develop?
- What new behaviours does the sports situation require?

Environment

- Where will the event take place?
- What will the crowd be like?
- What is the physical layout of the ground, pitch, etc?
- What is the style of the opposition?
- What is the ethos / culture of the opposition?
- At what level am I playing, e.g. promotion, relegation, fun, international?

One of the interesting aspects of personal change, whether it be in sport or any other walk of life, is how much (or little) we actually know about ourselves regarding our capabilities, values, beliefs, attitudes and identity. Certainly, from a sporting point of view, a healthy self-awareness (or realistic self-image, as some people call it) is a really useful component in improving both individual and team performance.

Many people who deal with personal change (whether in sport, family, business or education) start from the bottom of this model (i.e. the environment) and work up. This is not necessarily wrong, but it can have its limitations. If change only takes place at the visible level, i.e. the environment and the behaviour with some capabilities, the change may only be temporary rather than permanent. This is because we have not owned it and embedded it at a higher level as part of our attitudes and identity.

For example, if we achieve a notable victory which does not change or impact on our attitude regarding our true capabilities, the improvement in performance will be difficult to maintain. Equally, of course, if our attitude is that we are the best and will win every time, but our capabilities and behaviours do not support this attitude, we will end up losing. The art lies in having a balance between all five parts of the model.

In NLP this balance is called congruence. We are incongruent whenever what is happening at one of the levels does not match up with what is happening on the other levels. Some people call this state of congruence peace of mind. It is important to point out that this state is not the same as complacency, which can often mean that one or more of the five levels is not aligned, but the individual will not bother to do anything about it.

So in NLP, congruence is about being in rapport with ourselves, with all five levels aligned. In achieving improved sports performance, congruence can make the world of difference (as well as making us feel wonderful) and can often be the single factor that achieves the breakthrough or helps maintain progress and improvement.

The notion of congruence is vital to the issue of creating internal rewards. Achieving external rewards (e.g. money, fame, popularity, etc.) may well have its importance, but if external rewards cost us our personal worth or identity, then maybe they are too high a price to pay.

We need to aim for being able to achieve whatever external or material rewards we consider important, while at the same time being true to ourselves and having peace of mind. It is internal rewards that contribute to the latter. The activities that follow will help you to achieve appropriate internal rewards.

Activity

- Focus on the goal of creating a balanced state of mind.
- Go inside yourself and become aware of all your senses. Think about your goal and notice what you see, hear, feel, smell and taste.
- Concentrate on the first sense that comes to you (e.g. an image or sound) and intensify it.
- Bring in your other senses and link them all together.
- Continue until you have a clear sense of your goal with all of the five senses.
- When you have achieved this, check for congruency, through all five levels of the model.
- If there is a problem at any of the levels, make a note of it, as this is the level on which you need to work.
- If your goal is harmonious with all of the levels, enjoy the feeling and intensify it.

Activity

- Choose an internal reward that you would like to have for the first time.
- Think about how you would look, sound, feel and behave if you had that reward.
- Step into it and try it on. Actually experience how it looks, feels and sounds to have that reward.
- Change anything that doesn't feel right (stepping out of the experience, if necessary , to make the changes).
- Enjoy the experience, living it fully.
- Choose a particular signal for having the reward, i.e. how you know you've got it, what evidence you see, hear, feel, smell or taste.
- Step out of the experience.
- Activate your signal of having the reward, and notice how you feel.

Chapter 27

Banish Disempowering Beliefs

Throughout this book, beliefs have been mentioned as a key component in sports performance. If we do not actually believe deep down that we are good enough, no amount of physical training or externally applied motivation is going to make any difference. Therefore the difference between having empowering and disempowering beliefs is crucial.

It's better to have a strong mind than natural talent.
Eighty per cent of the game is in the mind.
David Lloyd

Anyone who has played sport at any level will have known someone who was very talented but, for some reason, did not really believe in themselves. This may have resulted in a wide variety of responses, e.g. not trying hard in practice, losing games or matches they should win, or appearing distracted at key moments. The other side of this coin is, of course, the sportsperson who has an inflated idea of their own ability. Their beliefs actually outweigh what they produce in performance. These people tend to have a wide range of excuses and people to blame for why nothing ever quite goes their way for some reason.

Both these types of sportspeople can have a negative effect in a team sport. In team squash the player who should win, but does not, makes life harder for their team-mates. In rugby or football the person who overrates themselves and will not pass when they should, can cause equally negative consequences.

Our beliefs may not be rational, although most of us operate as though our beliefs are absolutely true. An interesting sporting example was covered in the media in the summer of 1998. John Gregory, Aston Villa manager, was asked why he had failed in his first job at Portsmouth, where everything seemed designed for him to succeed. Part of his reply was that he knew exactly what he believed in, and expected everyone else to believe in the same thing and therefore respond in the same way. He discovered that this was not the case, and his first job in football management ended in failure. He has now put that experience to very positive use.

NLP shows that a belief is not necessarily right or wrong, but is simply an indicator of how we view the world. However, it is apparent that some beliefs are more empowering than others. People such as Daley Thomson, Steve Backley, Sally Gunnell, Neil Back, Rob Andrew, Michael Atherton have all demonstrated the effects of empowering beliefs. In spite of the negative situations they have found themselves in, or their negative previous experiences, they have come through both for themselves and the team. Other sportspeople tend to allow negative experiences to create negative beliefs about themselves, which ultimately disempower them.

In his book ***Sports Psychology In Action***, Richard J. Butler lists a number of consequences of such negative thinking and negative beliefs. They include:

- focusing on errors instead of successes
- performing badly because we expect to perform badly
- playing not to lose and restricting our performance to mediocrity so as to avoid risks
- trying to please others rather than focusing on our performance
- becoming tense
- losing confidence

As the case of John Gregory shows, most people expect others to share their own beliefs, and they get puzzled, frustrated or hostile when they do not. To understand someone's beliefs is *not the same as sharing them.* Some people actually recognise that one of their own beliefs lacks logic or is irrational, but seem to be unable to stop themselves acting on it as though it were absolutely true.The activities that follow are designed to create beliefs that are more empowering.

Activity

Practise using positive self-talk as a substitute for negative. This is based upon substituting your negative internal dialogue with a positive one.

For example:

- Instead of telling yourself: 'I always play badly at this ground', tell yourself: 'I will play excellently at this ground today.'
- Instead of telling yourself: 'I don't have the confidence to do this,' tell yourself: 'My confidence will see me through.'

Activity

This activity aims to change the flow of your attention and energy in a situation, in this case, lacking confidence in front of a large crowd. You can change the situation to any other where you feel you are affected by a negative belief.

Complete each sentence with whatever comes into your mind first.

Stage I

I lack confidence when I play in front of a large crowd

because ....
before ....
after ....
while ....
whenever ....
so that ....
if ....
although ....
in the same way that ....

/...continued overleaf

Stage II

I want to have confidence when I play in front of a large crowd

because ....

before ....

after ....

while ....

whenever ....

so that ....

if ....

although ....

in the same way that. ....

Stage III

I will be confident when playing in front of a large crowd

because ....

before ....

after ....

while ....

whenever ....

so that ....

if ....

although ....

in the same way that ....

Think carefully about how you have completed the sentences. Were there any surprises?

Activity

Anthony Robbins in his book *Awaken The Giant Within* suggests testing a disempowering belief by asking the following questions:

- How is this belief ridiculous or absurd?
- Was the person I learned this belief from worth modelling in this area?
- What will it ultimately cost me emotionally if I don't let go of this belief?
- What will it ultimately cost me in my relationships if I don't let go of this belief?
- What will it ultimately cost me physically if I don't let go of this belief?
- What will it ultimately cost me financially if I don't let go of this belief?
- What will it ultimately cost my family if I don't let go of this belief?

These questions can help break the negative states that can become attached to disempowering beliefs.

Activity

- Develop a visualisation (or picture in your mind) of your negative belief.
- Deliberately put a big frame around it.
- Place the framed picture in a specific spot where it is out of the way and it cannot interfere.
- Repeat this for other negative beliefs as you become aware of them (you may even like to build up an entire museum of discarded beliefs!).

Activity

Just before an event, place your negative belief into a mental black bag. Zip or button the black bag up and put it away out of sight until the event is over.

Activity

Do this activity with a friend or team-mate.

- Choose something that you believe you are *not* good at.
- Have your friend ask you these questions:
  - How do you know you're not good at it?
  - What causes you not to be good at it?
  - What does not being good at it mean?
  - What does that say to you?
  - What would happen if you didn't believe that?
  - So what new belief do you have now?
  - How can you apply this new belief in the future?
- Imagine yourself in a future sporting event, demonstrating this new belief.

Chapter 28

Deal With Difficulties

Every sportsperson, irrespective of his or her abilities, has at some point had a major problem to overcome. It might be recovery from a major injury, like Alan Shearer the England and Newcastle footballer, a lapse in form (which everyone gets at some stage), or dealing with a personal tragedy while still trying to compete.

Some health issues that may impact on sports performance are sexual problems, cigarettes, alcohol, drugs, surgery, insomnia, eating and diet disorders, childbirth, arthritis, cancer, irritable bowel syndrome, blood pressure, palpitations, sciatica, skin problems, ulcers and thyroid problems. Some of these health problems may be aggravated (or even caused) by playing particular sports.

The notion that some sportspeople have it easy is normally a false one. If someone survives without physical injury (although even at a fun or amateur level this is a rare occurrence) they may well have mental issues to deal with such as loss of confidence, insecurity about their own abilities, fear of the opponent, etc.

The interplay between physical and mental problems can be a fascinating one. Sometimes we may start out with a conventional injury but because it does not respond in the way that we would like it to, it starts to affect us mentally. On other occasions, our will to recover may be so strong that we start to play again before we should. Others may play on with an injury hoping that by ignoring it, it will just go away.

The capacity of the body to deal with pain is governed by the mind. Every sportsperson will know someone who allows each niggle to affect them while others seem to handle it completely differently. This also, of course, applies outside sports as well. Sir Ranulph Fiennes in his powerful and appropriately-titled book, *Mind Over Matter* quotes the French polar traveller, Jean-Louis Etienne as saying, 'When I get into a dangerous situation, my mind and my spirit go into a kind of "overdrive". I don't allow anger or frustration to absorb me. Travel in these conditions is seventy per cent mental.' Fiennes then goes on to say that 'such easy answers become less easy to apply to the mind when the brain is receiving constant pain messages from various parts of the body, which demand that the body stop *now*, not several hundred miles later.' He then explains how he, and others, use ideas like self-hypnosis, mantras, deliberately freewheeling in the mind, and concentration in order to deal with their pain issues.

When coping with pain or danger, the autonomic nervous system and the brain will respond immediately by releasing adrenaline and noradrenaline into the bloodstream. Adrenaline is a key factor in heightening awareness, improving concentration and dealing with the big moments effectively. Some of its effects can be measured by respiration rate, blood pressure, muscle tension, heart rate, biochemical indicators, sweating palms and galvanic skin response. Most sportspeople are aware in themselves (and often in others) of what their signals of arousal and anxiety are.

It is our own *perception* of the situation, rather than the situation itself, that will determine our level of anxiety and arousal. Jeremy Guscott and David Gower have often been accused of being too laid back, yet both were able to win matches or perform well, when all around them were acting like 'headless chickens'. The key is to recognise and establish our best personal level of arousal for ourselves.

Another difficulty that many sportspeople face is fear. Oddly, there are two things we fear: one is failure: the other is success. Both of these fears can be corrosive, often because sportspeople will not own up to them, or take ownership of them. The fear of failure can cause immense damage to self and peer-esteem and can create problems that can impact on other parts of life.

One reason that sportspeople may fear success is that it heightens the expectation of them, particularly in others, for the next time. These others could be friends, team-mates, colleagues at work, the manager, the coach, the club and, of course, the fans and general public. All of these create their own pressures and people will respond to them in different ways. For example, many sportspeople initially enjoy being famous, recognised in the street or sought out for interviews. At some point this novelty often wears off to be replaced by aloof detachment, suspicion and even hostility.

Whichever type of fear the sportsperson has, the end result can be the same: the lowering of performance levels. The reason for this is that we are programmed in all sorts of ways to deal with fear by running away from or avoiding it. NLP can help us to re-programme ourselves to tackle our fears head-on and overcome them.

Another difficulty that may confront all of us at some time is dealing with a loss of form. It is important to recognise it and to identify *why* it is taking place. Many players, managers and coaches are able to recognise the signs of a potential loss of form, almost before it starts to happen.

Normally the pattern is fairly clear. Often the loss of form is precipitated by a poor performance, which then triggers issues such as self-doubt, lack of confidence or the belief that it will get worse. This then creates the expectation that the next performance will be difficult in some way, and the mind sets out to look for the confirmation of this expectation (which the body obligingly produces).

What can be confusing about this process is that, although it runs inside the head, there are physical manifestations as well. Mental anxiety causes muscle tension, and the inability to relax or respond effectively, and it increases the chances of loss of performance or even injury.

One of the key issues in a loss of form is ownership. When faced with difficulties, many of us will not own our part in the issue, but will look instead for external factors to blame. Others will take the opposite approach and heap more and more blame on their own shoulders, irrespective of the evidence. Either way the result is the same: a further loss of form and performance.

It is simply not possible to play at a peak all the time. The art is to reduce the troughs that can occur in terms of both depth and duration, while also improving the peak levels of performance. The mind is capable of almost anything, including playing negative tricks and games. One bad innings, a couple of missed putts, a few poor first serves, all create the potential for a slide into poor performance. Fortunately, the mind is also capable of playing positive tricks and games, and we can have fun with these while overcoming our difficulties.

Activity

Choose a specific fear or anxiety, e.g. 'If I have to take a penalty shoot, I'll miss!'

- Imagine this fear *not* being fulfilled, i.e.. everything going well.
- Break the task down into smaller segments, see, hear, feel, smell and taste.
- Visualise being applauded at the end of the event. Even if you haven't won, visualise that you have performed excellently and beyond yourself. See, hear, feel, smell and taste yourself enjoying and deserving the applause.
- When actually performing, being totally focused in the present, carry out the actual skills in a step-by-step way, i.e. putting together the segments to build the whole event successfully.

Activity

Work with a partner.

- Tell your partner how *bad* you are at some aspect of your sport. Go into the full horror of it.
- After two minutes, let your partner do the same, telling you how bad he or she is at something.
- Clear your mind, take a deep breath, then take two minutes *convincing* your partner of a complete change, that you can now do the skill or behaviour extremely well. Be aware of your language, body language, feelings, etc.

Note: if this feels like acting, don't worry. Act 'as if' it were true, and see what happens.

- Do the same process with your partner.
- Talk about the changes that you feel.

Activity

This activity will help you to deal with pain through visualisation.

- Relax and close your eyes.
- Start deep (abdominal) breathing.
- See your tension as a waterfall or stream, flowing out of your body.
- With each inhalation visualise, feel and hear relaxation coming into your body and mind.
- If any parts of your body are particularly tense, move them slightly to remove all tension.
- Wherever the specific area of pain is, visualise, feel and hear the incoming breath going to that area and filling it with calmness, ease, and relaxed peace.
- With each exhalation visualise, feel, and hear the pain leaving that spot.
- If any emotions well up, allow them to come out through sighing, crying or whatever feels appropriate.
- Repeat the process for any other areas of pain.
- Focus on your breathing once again.
- Have a good stretch.
- Open your eyes and notice any changes in the level of pain.

NOTE: Obviously severe pain or injury should be dealt with by a doctor or physiotherapist.

Activity

This activity targets poor performance.

- Think of an occasion when you performed poorly.
- Analyse your thoughts, internal dialogue and visualisation in preparing for that event.
- Analyse your thoughts, internal dialogue and visualisation immediately before the event.
- Analyse the goals that you defined for that performance.
- Analyse your thoughts, internal dialogue and visualisation that you actually used during the event.
- Analyse the strategies you used for dealing with things going wrong.
- Analyse the thoughts, internal dialogue and visualisations you had after the event.
- Now think of a peak performance and carry out an analysis of it in the same way.
- Notice the differences, and use the information to help you to
  - develop strengths
  - eradicate weaknesses

Activity

- Establish the factors that are within your control when preparing and carrying out your sport.
- Develop methods, rituals, etc. for focusing on these controllable factors.

Activity

When something goes wrong, or doesn't quite work, use dissociation to separate you from your normal more associated responses (association and dissociation are covered in detail in chapter 4).

Glossary

Acute Exercise Short, sharp bursts of exercise normally of no more than 30 minutes duration.

Aerobic Exercise Continuous exercise with a sufficient supply of oxygen.

Anaerobic Exercise High intensity exercise where a period of recovery is required.

Anchoring The way that a stimulus or representation, which can be either internal or external, becomes connected to and triggers a response. Anchors can be established deliberately or occur naturally.

Associated Being inside one's own experiences and body looking out from own eyes.

As If Thinking or behaving as though something has actually taken place.

Backtracking Repeating back exactly what someone has said and how they said it.

Balanced Attention Placing the appropriate focus on what is happening both internally and externally at the present time.

Behaviour What sports people actually *do*, rather than what they are or think.

Burnout A state of physical and/or mental exhaustion produced by not being able to meet the demands of training or playing.

Capability The skills someone has to carry out a skill or task.

Chronic Exercise Overdoing exercise over a long period of time.

Cognitive-Behavioural Hypothesis The use of exercise to produce positive thoughts to counteract negative states.

Congruence The state of being at peace with oneself, with personal integrity and sincerity.

Conscious What we are aware of at a particular moment of time.

Coping Behaviour	Finding ways to challenge or deal with difficult situations.
Dissociated	Being outside one's own experience and body. Looking at self as if on a screen.
Exercise Addiction	Having an unhealthy dependence on a regular programme of exercise.
Exercise Adherence	Sticking to a given exercise programme.
Gustatory	The sense of taste (one of the representation systems).
Kinaesthetic	The sensation by which bodily position, weight, muscle tension and movement are perceived.
Learned Helplessness	A pattern of self-limitation which inhibits progress and trying new things.
Meta Program	The patterns of the way we structure experience through systematic and habitual filters.
Olfactory	The sense of smell.
Overtraining	Being unable to respond appropriately to the demands of the sport.
Physiological	To do with the body.
Staleness	Not being able to adapt to new situations in training or the sport.
State	How we are at a particular time.
Training Stress Syndrome	Starts with elements of staleness and overtraining and finishes in burnout.
Unconscious	Everything that is at that moment outside the conscious mind.
Visualization	Being able to see pictures and images in the mind.

Bibliography

This bibliography is split into two sections.

The first is composed of NLP books that can have sporting applications. The second is a selection of sports psychology books or articles that would be of interest to someone wishing to go deeper into the subject.

NLP or Related Books

Bandler, R, *Using Your Brain For A Change,* Real People Press, Utah, USA, 1985.

Bandler, R, & Grinder, J, *Reframing, Neuro-Linguistic Programming And The Transformation Of Meaning,* Real People Press, Utah, USA, 1982.

Bandler, R. & McDonald, W, *An Insider's Guide To Sub-Modalities,* Meta Publications, Cupertino, California, USA, 1988.

Bodenhamer, Bob & Hall, L Michael, *Time-Lining: Patterns For Adventuring In "Time",* Crown House Publishing, Carmarthen, Wales, UK, 1997.

Bolduc, HL, *Self Hypnosis: Creating Your Own Destiny,* Adventures in To Time, Virginia, 1992.

Butler & Hope, *Manage Your Mind,* Oxford University Press, Oxford, UK, 1995.

Charvet, SR, *Words That Change Minds* Kendall/Hunt Publishing, Iowa, USA, 1996.

Covey, S, *Seven Habits Of Highly Effective People,* Simon and Schuster, London, UK, 1989.

Dilts, R, & Epstein, T, *Tools For Dreamers,* Meta Publications, Cupertino, California, USA, 1991.

Dilts, R, *Changing Belief Systems With NLP,* Meta Publications, Cupertino, California, USA, 1990.

Dilts, R, Grinder, J, Bandler, R, & DeLozier, J, *Neuro-Linguistic Programming: Vol I The Study of Subjective Experience,* Meta Publications, Cupertino, California, USA, 1980.

Dennison, P, Dennison G, *Brain Gym, Teacher's Edition*, Edu-Kinesthetics, Ventura, California, USA, 1989.

Ford, M, *Motivating Humans*, Sage Publications, Newbury Park, California, USA, 1992.

Gardner, H, with Krechevsky, M, *Multiple Intelligences: The Theory In Practice,* Basic Books, New York, USA, 1993.

Goleman, D, *Emotional Intelligence*, Bloomsbury Press, London, UK, 1995.

Guyonnaud, Dr JP, with Sciuto, G, *Self Hypnosis: Step By Step,* Souvenir Press, London, UK, 1989.

Hanaford, C, *The Dominance Factor*, Great Ocean Publishers, Arlington, VA, USA, 1997.

Hooper, J, & Terisi, D, *The Three Pound Universe: The Brain From Chemistry Of The Mind To New Frontiers Of The Soul,* Dell Publishing, New York, USA, 1986.

Kermani, Dr Kai, *Autogenic Training*, Souvenir Press, London, UK, 1996.

James, T, & Woodsmall, W, *Time Line Therapy And The Basis Of Personality*, Meta Publications, Cupertino, California, USA, 1988.

James, T, *The Secret Of Creating Your Future,* Advanced Neuro Dynamics, Honolulu, Hawaii, USA, 1989.

Jensen, E, *Super Teaching: Master Strategies For Building Student Success,* Turning Point For Teachers, San Diego, California, USA, 1994.

Jensen, E, *The Learning Brain*, Turning Point For Teachers, San Diego, California, USA, 1994.

Kostere, K, & Malatesta, L, *Maps, Models And The Structure Of Reality*, Metamorphous Press, Portland, Oregon, USA, 1990.

Kotulak, R, *Unravelling Hidden Mysteries Of The Brain*, Chicago Tribune 11 – 16 April 1993, USA, 1993.

Locke, E, & Latham, GP, *Work Motivation And Satisfaction: Light At The End Of The Tunnel*, Psychological Science I, 240 –46, USA, 1990.

Lombardi, V, *Run To Daylight*, Tempo Books, New York, USA, 1963.

Lozanov, G, *Suggestology And Outlines Of Suggestopedy*, Gordon and Breach, New York, USA, 1978.

Lozanov, G, "On Some Problems Of The Anatomy, Physiology And Biochemistry Of Cerebral Activities In The Global – Artistic Approach In Modern Suggestopedagogic Training", *The Journal Of The Society For Accelerative Learning And Teaching* 16, 2, 101 – 16, 1991.

Maguire, J, *Care And Feeding Of The Brain*, Doubleday, New York, USA, 1990.

Ostrander, S, & Schroder, L, with Ostrander, N, *Super Learning 2000*, Souvenir Press, London, UK, 1994.

Robbins, A, *Awaken The Giant Within*, Simon and Schuster, Englewood Cliffs, New Jersey, USA, 1992.

Rose, C, & Tracy, B, *Accelerated Learning Techniques*, Nightingale Conant, Niles, Illinois, USA, 1995.

Seymour, J, & O'Connor, J, *Introducing NLP*, Harper Collins, London, UK, 1990.

Varca, PE, "An Analysis Of Home And Away Game Performance Of Male Basketball Teams." *Journal of Sports Psychology* 2, 245-257, 1980.

Waitley, D, *The Psychology of Winning* Tape, Nightingales Conant, Illinois, USA, 1995.

Books And Articles On Sports Psychology And Related Topics

Bandura, A, "Self-Efficacy: Towards A Unifying Theory Of Behavioural Change", *Psychology Review* 84 191-215, 1973.

Butler, RJ, *Sports Psychology In Action*, Butterworth-Heinemann, Oxford, UK,1996.

Clark, LV, "Effect Of Mental Practice On The Development Of A Certain Motor Skill", *Research Quarterly*, 31, 560-569, 1960.

Cox, RH, *Sports Psychology, Concepts And Applications*, WCB, Brown and Benchmark, Iowa, USA, 1994.

Endler, NS, "The Interaction Model Of Anxiety: Some Possible Implications" in DM Landers & RW Christina (Eds) *Psychology Of Motor Behaviour And Sport*, Human Kinetics, Champaign, Ilinois, USA, 1977.

Fiennes, R, *Mind Over Matter*, Mandarin Books, London, UK, 1993.

Gallway, WT, *The Inner Game Of Tennis*, Pan Books, London, UK, 1975.

Goldberg, AS, *Sports Slump Busting*, Human Kinetics, Champaign, Illinois, USA, 1998.

Hall, CR, Rodgers, WM, & Barr, KA, "The Use Of Imagery By Athletes In Selected Sports", *The Sports Psychologist* 4 1-10, 1990.

Hemery, D, *Sporting Excellence*, Collins Willow, London, UK, 1991.

Harter, S, "Effective Motivation Reconsidered: Towards A Developmental Model", *Human Development* 21 34-64, 1978.

Locke, EA, Shaw, KM, Saari, LM & Latham, G, "Goal Setting And Task Performance: 1969-80", *Psychology Bulletin* 90 125-152, 1981.

Loehr, Dr JE & McLauglin, DJ, *Mental Toughness: Training To Achieve And Command The Ideal Performance State*, Nightingale-Conant, Chicago, Illinois, USA, 1990.

Mailer, N, *The Fight*, Penguin Books, London, UK, 1975.

Nicholls, JG, "Conceptions Of Ability And Achievement Motivation", in IR Ames & C Ames (Eds) *Research On Motivation In Education: Student Motivation (Vol I)*, New York, Academic Press, USA, 1984.

Orlick, T, *In Pursuit Of Excellence*, Leisure Press, Champaign, Illinois, USA, 1990.

Syer, J & Connolly, C, *Sporting Body, Sporting Mind*, Sportspages, London, UK, 1987.

Rodber, T, *Mental Physical Fitness For Sport*, Hodder and Stoughton, London, UK, 1996.

Vealey, RS, "Conceptualisation Of Sport Confidence And Competitive Orientation: Preliminary Investigations And Instrument Development", *Journal Of Sports Psychology*, 8 221-246, 1986.

Crown House Publishing Limited

Crown Buildings,
Bancyfelin,
Carmarthen, Wales, UK, SA33 5ND.
Telephone: +44 (0) 1267 211880
Facsimile: +44 (0) 1267 211882
e-mail: bshine@crownhouse.co.uk
Website: www.crownhouse.co.uk

We trust you enjoyed this title from our range of bestselling books for professional and general readership. All our authors are professionals of many years' experience, and all are highly respected in their own field. We choose our books with care for their content and character, and for the value of their contribution of both new and updated material to their particular field. Here is a list of all our other publications.

***Change Management Excellence**: Putting NLP To Work In The 21st Century*
by Martin Roberts PhD — Hardback — £25.00

***Dreaming Realities:** A Spiritual System To Create Inner Alignment Through Dreams*
by John Overdurf & Julie Silverthorn — Paperback — £9.99

***Doing It With Pete:** The Lighten Up Slimming Fun Book*
by Pete Cohen & Judith Verity — Paperback — £9.99

***Ericksonian Approaches**: A Comprehensive Manual*
by Rubin Battino & Thomas L South PhD — Hardback — £25.00

***Figuring Out People**: Design Engineering With Meta-Programs*
by Bob G. Bodenhamer & L. Michael Hall — Paperback — £12.99

***Gold Counselling, Second Edition**: The Practical Psychology With NLP*
by Georges Philips & Lyn Buncher — Paperback — £16.99

***Grieve No More, Beloved**: The Book Of Delight*
by Ormond McGill — Hardback — £9.99

***Hypnotherapy Training In The UK:** An Investigation Into The Development Of Clinical Hypnosis Training Post-1971*
by Shaun Brookhouse — Spiralbound — £9.99

***Influencing With Integrity:** Management Skills For Communication & Negotiation*
by Genie Z Laborde — Paperback — £12.50

***Instant Relaxation:** How To Reduce Stress At Work, At Home And In Your Daily Life*
by L. Michael Hall with Debra Lederer — Paperback — £8.99

***The Magic Of Mind Power:** Awareness Techniques For The Creative Mind*
by Duncan McColl — Paperback — £8.99

A Multiple Intelligences Road To An ELT Classroom
by Michael Berman — Paperback — £19.99

Multiple Intelligences Poster Set
by Jenny Maddern — Nine posters — £19.99

The New Encyclopedia Of Stage Hypnotism
by Ormond McGill — Hardback — £29.99

***Now It's YOUR Turn For Success!** Training And Motivational Techniques For Direct Sales And Multi-Level Marketing*
by Richard Houghton and Janet Kelly — Paperback — £9.99

Peace Of Mind Is A Piece Of Cake by Michael Mallows & Joseph Sinclair	Paperback	£8.99
The POWER Process*: An NLP Approach To Writing* by Sid Jacobson & Dixie Elise Hickman	Paperback	£12.99
Precision Therapy: *A Professional Manual Of Fast And Effective Hypnoanalysis Techniques* by Duncan McColl PhD	Paperback	£15.00
Rapid Cognitive Therapy: *The Professional Therapists' Guide To Rapid Change Work* by Georges Philips & Terrence Watts	Paperback	£20.00
Scripts & Strategies In Hypnotherapy by Roger P. Allen	Hardback	£19.99
The Secrets Of Magic: *Communicational Excellence For The 21st Century* by L. Michael Hall	Paperback	£14.99
Seeing The Unseen*: A Past Life Revealed Through Hypnotic Regression* by Ormond McGill	Paperback	£12.99
Slimming With Pete: *Taking The Weight Off Body AND Mind* by Pete Cohen & Judith Verity	Paperback	£9.99
Smoke-Free And No Buts! by Geoff Ibbotson & Ann Williamson	Paperback	£5.99
Solution States*: A Course In Solving Problems In Business With The Power Of NLP* by Sid Jacobson	Paperback	£12.99
The Sourcebook Of Magic*: A Comprehensive Guide To NLP Techniques* by L. Michael Hall & Barbara Belnap	Paperback	£14.99
The Spirit Of NLP*: The Process, Meaning And Criteria For Mastering NLP* by L. Michael Hall	Paperback	£12.99
Time-Lining*: Patterns For Adventuring In "Time"* by Bob G. Bodenhamer & L. Michael Hall	Paperback	£14.99
The User's Manual For The Brain: *The Complete Manual For Neuro-Linguistic Programming Practitioner Certification* by Bob G. Bodenhamer & L. Michael Hall	A4 binder	£35.00
Vibrations For Health And Happiness*: Everyone's Easy Guide To Stress-free Living* by Tom Bolton	Paperback	£9.99

Order form

*******Special offer: 4 for the price of 3!!!*******

Buy 3 books & we'll give you a 4th title - FREE!

(free title will be book of lowest value)

Qty	Title	Qty	Title
—	Change Management Excellence	—	Peace Of Mind Is A Piece Of Cake
—	Doing It With Pete	—	The POWER Process
—	Dreaming Realities	—	Precision Therapy
—	Ericksonian Approaches	—	Rapid Cognitive Therapy
—	Figuring Out People	—	Scripts & Strategies In Hypnotherapy
—	Gold Counselling™ Second Edition	—	The Secrets Of Magic
—	Grieve No More, Beloved	—	Seeing The Unseen
—	Hypnotherapy Training In The UK	—	Slimming With Pete
—	Influencing With Integrity	—	Smoke-Free And No Buts!
—	Instant Relaxation	—	Solution States
—	The Magic Of Mind Power	—	The Sourcebook Of Magic
—	A Multiple Intelligences Road To An ELT Classroom	—	The Spirit Of NLP
—	Multiple Intelligences Poster Set	—	Sporting Excellence
—	New Encyclopedia Of Stage Hypnotism	—	Time-Lining
—	Now It's YOUR Turn For Success!	—	The User's Manual For The Brain
		—	Vibrations For Health And Happiness

Postage and packing

UK:	£2.50 for one book
	£4.50 for two or more books
Europe:	£3.50 per book
Rest of the world	£4.50 per book

My details:

Name: Mr/Mrs/Ms/Other (please specify) ....

Address: ....

....

....

Postcode: ....Daytime tel: ....

I wish to pay by:

☐ Amex ☐ Visa ☐ Mastercard ☐ Switch – Issue no./Start date:

....

Card number:..Expiry date:..

Name on card:..Signature:..

☐ cheque/postal order payable to **AA Books**

Please send me the following catalogues:

☐ Accelerated Learning (Teaching Resources)
☐ Accelerated Learning (Personal Growth)
☐ Neuro-Linguistic Programming
☐ NLP Video Library – hire (UK only)
☐ NLP Video Library – sales
☐ Ericksonian Hypnotherapy
☐ Classical Hypnosis
☐ Gestalt Therapy
☐ Psychotherapy/Counselling
☐ Employment Development
☐ Business
☐ Freud
☐ Jung
☐ Transactional Analysis
☐ Parenting
☐ Special Needs

Please fax/send to:

The Anglo American Book Company,
FREEPOST SS1340
Crown Buildings, Bancyfelin,
Carmarthen, West Wales,
United Kingdom, SA33 4ZZ,
Tel: +44 (0) 1267 211880/211886 Fax: +44 (0) 1267 211882
or e-mail your order to:
books@anglo-american.co.uk